Potatoes

GENERAL EDITOR
CHUCK WILLIAMS

RECIPES
DIANE ROSSEN WORTHINGTON

PHOTOGRAPHY
ALLAN ROSENBERG

TIME
LIFE
BOOKS

Time-Life Books is a division of Time Life Inc.
Time-Life is a trademark of Time Warner Inc. U.S.A.

President and CEO: John M. Fahey, Jr.
President, Time-Life Books: John D. Hall

TIME-LIFE CUSTOM PUBLISHING

Vice President and Publisher: Terry Newell
Sales Director: Frances C. Mangan
Editorial Director: Donia Steele

WILLIAMS-SONOMA
Founder/Vice-Chairman: Chuck Williams

WELDON OWEN INC.
President: John Owen
Publisher: Wendely Harvey
Managing Editor: Laurie Wertz
Consulting Editor: Norman Kolpas
Copy Editor: Sharon Silva
Design/Editorial Assistant: Janique Poncelet
Design: John Bull, The Book Design Company
Production: Stephanie Sherman, James Obata,
    Mick Bagnato
Co-Editions Director: Derek Barton
Co-Editions Production Manager (US): Tarji Mickelson
Food Photographer: Allan Rosenberg
Additional Food Photography: Allen V. Lott
Primary Food & Prop Stylist: Sandra Griswold
Food Stylist: Heidi Gintner
Assistant Food Stylist: Danielle Di Salvo
Glossary Illustrations: Alice Harth

The Williams-Sonoma Kitchen Library
conceived and produced by Weldon Owen Inc.
814 Montgomery St., San Francisco, CA 94133

In collaboration with Williams-Sonoma
3250 Van Ness Ave., San Francisco, CA 94109

Production by Mandarin Offset, Hong Kong
Printed in China

A Note on Weights and Measures:
All recipes include customary U.S. and metric
measurements. Metric conversions are based on
a standard developed for these books and have
been rounded off. Actual weights may vary.

A Weldon Owen Production

Copyright © 1993 Weldon Owen Inc.
Reprinted in 1994; 1994; 1994; 1994; 1995; 1995;
    1996

Library of Congress
Cataloging-in-Publication Data:

Worthington, Diane Rossen.
    Potatoes / general editor, Chuck Williams ;
recipes, Diane Rossen Worthington ;
photography, Allan Rosenberg.
        p.   cm. — (Williams-Sonoma kitchen library)
    Includes index.
    ISBN 0-7835-0275-3 ;
    ISBN 0-7835-0276-1 (lib. bdg.)
    1. Cookery (Potatoes)   I. Williams, Chuck.
II. Title.   III. Series.
TX803.P8W67   1994
641.6'521—dc20   93-28231
                                      CIP

Contents

ROASTED & BAKED 17

FRIED, SAUTÉED & GRILLED 63

MASHED, BOILED & STEAMED 83

SALADS 93

INTRODUCTION

Few individual vegetables merit a book of their own. But the humble potato stands apart from the rest of the vegetable world.

Rich, earthy, flavorful and filling, potatoes satisfy like few other foods. And their taste, texture, and the vast number of varieties available make potatoes endlessly adaptable to virtually every cooking method, manner of seasoning and kind of meal. Looking for the perfect accompaniment to a main course? Plan on potatoes. Want a tempting appetizer or a flavorful luncheon dish? Potatoes are a logical choice. Can't decide what to make yourself for dinner? Bake a potato. There's nothing better. (But please be sure to bake it in its natural skin alone, rather than oven-steaming it in a foil wrapper!)

From perfect baked potatoes (you'll find the key on page 9) to the most stylish potato creations, this book celebrates everybody's favorite vegetable in all its variety, including sweet potatoes and yams, cousins of the potato that deserve attention year-round rather than just during the holiday season. The introductory pages will guide you through the basics of potato cookery, from selecting and storing potatoes to baking, mashing, frying, topping and saucing them. The 44 recipes that follow, each illustrated with a full-color photograph, are organized by cooking method for ease of reference: roasted and baked potato dishes; fried, sautéed and grilled recipes; mashed, boiled and steamed potatoes; and potato salads.

Many of these recipes are good examples of the sensible approach to nutrition and diet that has blossomed in recent years. Low in fat and high in the complex carbohydrates potatoes naturally offer, the recipes can be as good for you as they are delicious. So whether you're watching what you eat at the moment or have always led a life of healthful moderation, I'm sure you'll find within this volume new inspiration to cook and enjoy everyone's favorite vegetable.

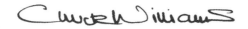

EQUIPMENT

From purées to French fries, gratins to baked potatoes,
a range of simple tools makes perfection easy to attain

Boiling, steaming, baking, frying: These are the simple ways in which we cook potatoes, and they call for the most basic kitchen equipment, from knives and peelers to pots and pans, from spoons and spatulas to baking dishes.

A few additional tools, however, will speed the work of preparing potatoes in quantity. For example, if a recipe calls for cutting potatoes into uniform slices or shreds, an old-fashioned hand-operated French mandoline performs the task with a speed and efficiency comparable to a state-of-the-art food processor. A ricer or food mill yields perfect potato purées with just a squeeze or turn of the handle. And an automatic deep-fryer eliminates much of the mess and uncertainty associated with deep-frying, making perfect French fries and potato chips more accessible to the home cook than ever before.

1. Automatic Deep-Fat Fryer
Temperature- and timer-controlled, enclosed appliance allows accurate deep-frying free of splatters and odors. Alternatively, use a deep, heavy pot and a deep-frying thermometer.

2. Assorted Kitchen Tools
A variety of simple tools assist in potato cookery, including: scrub brush, for cleaning potatoes; wooden spoons and wire whisk, for general-purpose stirring; spatula, for turning panfried potatoes; deep-frying thermometer, to ensure accurate oil temperature.

3. Baking Sheet
For holding baked or stuffed potatoes in the oven.

4. Mandoline
Sturdy, stainless-steel apparatus quickly slides whole or halved potatoes up and down its surface for fast, accurate slicing or shredding by hand.

5. Colander
For washing and draining potatoes. Choose stainless steel; enameled-steel colanders are also good choices.

6. Gratin Dishes
For holding oven-baked potatoes. Available in a variety of sizes and shapes; select heavy-duty glazed porcelain, stoneware, earthenware or glass.

7. Soufflé Dish
Circular, deep, straight-sided dish of heavy-duty glazed porcelain or glass, for baking soufflés or casseroles.

8. Potato Masher
For simple, quick mashing of potatoes in small to moderate quantities. Choose a sturdy masher made of stainless steel.

9. Ricer
Sturdy, hinged stainless-steel apparatus forces boiled potatoes through small holes, producing fine-textured, smooth mashed potatoes and purées.

10. Frying Pan
Choose good-quality, heavy stainless steel, thick aluminum, cast iron or heavy enameled steel for rapid browning and frying of potatoes. Flared sides facilitate turning and allow moisture to escape more easily for crisp results.

11. Skimmer
Wide bowl and fine mesh ensure easy, neat removal of fried potatoes from hot oil.

12. Strainer
For removing and draining boiled potatoes.

13. Steamer Basket
Petaled, flowerlike shape enables the basket to expand or contract to fit saucepans of various sizes, to hold potatoes above the level of simmering liquid during steaming. Small post in center is used to lift the basket out of the pan once the food is cooked.

14. Stockpot and Saucepan
For all-purpose stove-top cooking of potatoes.

15. Food Mill
Hand-turned crank forces boiled potatoes through one of two disks for coarser or finer purées.

16. Grater/Shredder
Sturdy, stainless-steel tool for grating or shredding potatoes by hand.

17. Kitchen Knives
For general paring, peeling, cutting, slicing and chopping of potatoes. Choose sturdy knives with sharp, stainless-steel blades securely attached to sturdy handles that feel comfortable in the hand.

18. Peelers
Curved, slotted swiveling blade thinly strips away the peel from potatoes and other vegetables. Small slotted blade peels small potatoes or cuts thin strips of zest from citrus fruits.

19. Cutting Board
Choose one made of tough but resilient white acrylic, which is nonporous and cleans easily; wooden cutting boards may also be used for potatoes and other vegetables.

20. Slotted Spoon
For all-purpose stirring and for lifting out and draining boiled potatoes.

POTATO BASICS

A simple guide to the world of potatoes, including advice on cooking, selection and storage

From region to region and nation to nation, the kinds of potatoes grown and sold and the names used for them vary widely. Nevertheless, potatoes can be divided into several basic categories, for which the following terms are used throughout this book:

Baking potato. Large potatoes with thick brown skins, whose dry, mealy textures when cooked make them ideal for baking, mashing or deep-frying. Also known as russet or Idaho potatoes.

White potato. Generally medium-sized potatoes with thin tan skins, whose textures when cooked—finer than baking potatoes but coarser than waxy yellow varieties—make them a good all-purpose choice.

Yellow potato. Any of a variety of thin-skinned potatoes with yellow-tinged, waxy flesh well suited to steaming, boiling, roasting or sautéing.

Red potato. Crisp, waxy, white-fleshed potato with thin red skin. Ideal for steaming, boiling and roasting.

New potato. Refers to any variety of potato harvested in early summer when small and immature, resulting in more tender, sweeter flesh best appreciated steamed, boiled or roasted. Red-skinned new potatoes are the most common new potatoes found in the market.

Sweet potato. Not a true potato, though resembling it in form, this tuberous vegetable has light to deep red skin and pale yellow to orange flesh prized for its sweetness when cooked. The light-skinned variety is the most common.

Yam-type sweet potato. True yams are large tuberous vegetables native to the Caribbean. Elsewhere, though, the term *yam* is sometimes applied to the dark-skinned variety of sweet potato with sweet, deep orange flesh.

SELECTING AND STORING POTATOES

Whatever type of potato you buy, always choose firm, well-shaped ones free of blemishes, bruises, discolorations or sprouting eyes. Especially avoid those with green spots, which indicate the presence of a toxic alkaloid called solanine that results from exposure to light. To make sure that small raw potatoes truly are "new" potatoes, gently rub their skins; being immature, the skins should come off easily.

Do not wash potatoes before storing. Moisture can cause spoilage. Place in a vegetable bin or wrap loosely in brown paper; avoid plastic bags, which trap moisture. Store in the dark, at cool room temperature between 45°–50°F (8°–10°C); lower temperatures will blacken them. Cook most potatoes within 10 days of purchase, new potatoes within 2–3 days.

Baking potato

Yam-type sweet potato

Yellow potato

New potato

White potato

Sweet potato

Red potato

Basic Baked Potatoes

Choose medium-sized baking potatoes for the best texture and the most even cooking. Rubbing the potatoes with vegetable oil yields a crisp skin. For an extra-crisp skin, bake at 450°F (230°C).

4 baking potatoes, about ½ lb (250 g) each, unpeeled
4 teaspoons vegetable oil

Preheat an oven to 425°F (220°C). Scrub the potatoes to remove all dirt, then dry thoroughly with a kitchen towel. Prick the skin in a few places with a fork. Rub each potato with 1 teaspoon of the oil to coat evenly. Place the potatoes on an ungreased baking sheet in the middle of the oven.

Bake until tender when pierced with a knife or skewer, about 1 hour. The potatoes should be cooked through and slightly crisp on the outside.

If the baked potatoes are to be used as the base for stuffed potatoes or another potato dish, proceed as directed in those recipes. If serving immediately, grasp each potato with a potholder and cut it down the center lengthwise to reach halfway through its depth. Then pinch the sides together so the potato pulp plumps in the middle and the steam is released. Serve at once.

Serves 4

TOPPINGS FOR BAKED POTATOES

Spicy tomato salsa *(recipe on page 11)*
Red pepper aïoli *(recipe on page 11)*
Pesto *(recipe on page 10)*
Sun-dried tomato pesto *(recipe on page 10)*
Roasted garlic purée *(recipe on pages 10–11),* sour cream and chopped fresh herbs
Butter mixed with minced fresh herbs
Caviar and sour cream
Assorted mustards such as coarse-grain, Dijon or herb-flavored Dijon
Grated sharp Cheddar cheese or crumbled feta or fresh goat cheese

Pesto

Pesto—a pungent sauce of basil and olive oil—is a versatile condiment delicious on baked, steamed or mashed potatoes.

2 cloves garlic
2 cups (2 oz/60 g) fresh basil leaves (about 2 bunches)
½ cup (½ oz/15 g) fresh parsley leaves
2 tablespoons pine nuts
½ cup (4 fl oz/125 ml) olive oil
¼ teaspoon freshly ground pepper
¾ cup (3 oz/90 g) freshly grated Parmesan cheese

*F*it a food processor with the metal blade and start the motor. Alternatively, use a blender. Add the garlic cloves and process until puréed.

Add the basil and parsley and process to chop finely. Add the pine nuts and process to chop finely. With the blades turning, slowly pour in the olive oil in a fine, steady stream. Add the pepper and cheese and process until well blended, stopping the motor as needed to scrape down the sides. Taste and adjust the seasoning.

Store refrigerated in a tightly covered container for up to 5 days.

Makes about 1¼ cups (10 fl oz/310 ml)

Pesto

Sun-Dried
Tomato Pesto

Sun-Dried Tomato Pesto

Simple mashed or baked potatoes are enlivened by this rustic tomato condiment. Or try it in place of the basil pesto in the recipe for pesto-baked wedges (page 31). A blender can be used, although it may not combine the ingredients as efficiently as a food processor.

1 clove garlic
½ cup (4 oz/125 g) coarsely chopped sun-dried
   tomatoes packed in olive oil, well drained
2 tablespoons chopped fresh basil
¼ teaspoon salt
⅛ teaspoon freshly ground pepper
2 tablespoons olive oil
2 tablespoons hot water, if needed

*S*tart the motor of a food processor fitted with the metal blade. Add the garlic and process until minced. Add the tomatoes, basil, salt, pepper and olive oil and process until a thick paste forms. If the paste is too thick, thin it with the hot water or a little more oil.

Store refrigerated in a tightly covered container for up to 1 week.

Makes about ½ cup (4 fl oz/125 ml)

Roasted Garlic Purée

Roasted garlic has a mellow, nutty flavor that complements potatoes. Swirl this rich purée into mashed potatoes or creamy potato purées.

2 whole heads garlic

*P*reheat an oven to 425°F (220°C).

Using a sharp knife, cut off the top one-fourth of each garlic head. Gently score the head around its middle, cutting through a few layers of the papery skin. Pull off any loose skin from the top half of the head, trying not to remove every shred. (This will make it easier to squeeze out the cooked cloves later.) Tightly wrap each head in a piece of aluminum foil and place on a baking sheet or in a small baking dish.

Bake until the garlic is soft when pierced with a knife, 45–60 minutes. Remove from the oven and let cool. Using your fingers, squeeze the soft garlic pulp into a small bowl. Store tightly covered in the refrigerator for up to 3 days.

Makes about 2 tablespoons

Red Pepper Aïoli

Use this garlicky, pale red mayonnaise to flavor potato salad or mashed potatoes, or to top baked potatoes. A canned whole pimiento can be used in place of the freshly roasted bell pepper.

1 red bell pepper (capsicum)
4 cloves garlic
1 cup (8 fl oz/250 ml) mayonnaise
salt
white pepper
pinch of cayenne pepper

*R*oast and peel the bell pepper (see glossary, page 106). Remove the seeds and ribs and chop the pepper.

Start the motor of a blender or of a food processor fitted with the metal blade. Add the garlic and process until puréed. Add the roasted pepper and process until well blended. Add the mayonnaise and process just until mixed. Add salt and white pepper to taste and the cayenne pepper. Taste and adjust the seasoning.

Store refrigerated in a tightly covered container for up to 1 week.

Makes about 1¼ cups (10 fl oz/310 ml)

Spicy Tomato Salsa

The oils in chili peppers are very potent. When working with peppers, always wear rubber gloves, never touch your eyes or other sensitive areas, and wash the cutting surface and knife immediately afterward. This salsa makes a light, flavorful topping for baked potatoes or crisp potato skins.

2 large tomatoes, peeled, seeded and finely chopped
1 fresh jalapeño or serrano chili pepper, seeded and finely chopped
1 tablespoon finely chopped fresh cilantro (fresh coriander)
½ small red (Spanish) onion, finely chopped
1 small clove garlic, minced
1 teaspoon fresh lime juice
½ teaspoon salt
pinch of freshly ground pepper

*I*n a bowl combine all the ingredients and, using a spoon, mix well. Taste and adjust the seasoning. Store refrigerated in a tightly covered container for up to 5 days.

Makes about 2 cups (16 fl oz/500 ml)

Red Pepper Aïoli

Roasted Garlic Purée

Spicy Tomato Salsa

11

Basic Mashed Potatoes

Everyone has their favorite type of mashed potatoes. Some prefer them fluffy rather than creamy, while others like them smooth rather than lumpy.

Any type of potato can be used for mashed potatoes. White, red and yellow potatoes result in a creamy consistency; baking potatoes produce a fluffier mashed potato.

The best way to make smooth, creamy mashed potatoes is not to mash them at all, but to put them through a ricer. A food mill also works nicely. Some people prefer to use a potato masher, which results in lumpy, fluffier mashed potatoes. Even a fork will work if you're in a pinch. Just be sure not to use a food processor or you will end up with a gluey mass.

Make sure to dry the potatoes well after cooking by draining them thoroughly and then returning them to the pan over high heat for 1–2 minutes, turning them so they do not scorch. This step will ensure a creamy rather than watery mashed potato.

If you must hold the mashed potatoes before serving, keep them warm in the top pan of a double boiler or in a heatproof bowl placed over (but not touching) simmering water for up to 1 hour. This prevents them from drying out.

Mashed potatoes are delicious topped with pesto or sundried tomato pesto (recipes on page 10), a favorite cheese, or plain or herb-flavored butter.

2 lb (1 kg) white, red, yellow-fleshed or baking potatoes, peeled and cut into 2-inch (5-cm) pieces
1 teaspoon salt, plus salt to taste
¼ cup (2 oz/60 g) unsalted butter, cut into small pieces
¾ cup (6 fl oz/180 ml) half-and-half, heated
white pepper

To remove excess starch, place the potatoes in a large bowl and add water to cover; let stand for 5 minutes, then drain.

Fill a large pot three-fourths full with water and bring to a boil. Add the 1 teaspoon salt and the potatoes and cook until tender when pierced with a fork, about 15 minutes. Drain well in a colander and return to the pot over high heat to dry, turning to prevent scorching, until all the moisture evaporates, 1–2 minutes.

If you are serving the mashed potatoes immediately, hold a ricer over a large bowl. If you are keeping the mashed potatoes for a while before serving, hold the ricer over the top pan of a 2-qt (2-l) double boiler or a heatproof bowl placed over (but not touching) hot water. Put the potato cubes through the ricer. Add the butter to the bowl and slowly add the half-and-half, a little at a time, stirring constantly with a large spoon, until the potatoes are very creamy but not soupy. Season to taste with salt and white pepper. Transfer to a warmed serving dish.

Serves 4

Using a ricer
For smooth, creamy mashed potatoes, put boiled potatoes in a ricer and press down on the handle to force them through the tool's tiny holes.

Using a food mill
Fit a food mill with the fine or coarse puréeing disk, depending upon desired texture. Put boiled potatoes into the mill and turn the handle to force the potatoes through the disk.

Using a masher
For the widest range of control over the finished results—from home-style lumpy potatoes to fluffy purées—mash by hand with a sturdy potato masher.

Hash Brown Potatoes

Use the small holes of a shredder for shredding the potatoes, and a nonstick frying pan for ease in turning. If you like, just before cooking the potatoes, season them with herbs, spices or other ingredients that complement whatever else you are serving. For instance, use ground cumin and minced fresh chilies for a Mexican flavor, or minced fresh basil and garlic for a Mediterranean touch. Serve with scrambled eggs, omelets, frittatas or any egg dish of your choice. Peeling the potatoes is optional.

1 lb (500 g) baking potatoes, peeled and finely
   shredded
½ teaspoon salt
pinch of freshly ground pepper
2 tablespoons unsalted butter
1 tablespoon olive oil

Place the shredded potatoes in a bowl, add water to cover and let stand for 5 minutes to remove excess starch. Drain the potatoes and dry thoroughly with a kitchen towel, squeezing out all excess water. Place the potatoes in a bowl, add the salt and pepper and mix well.

In a large nonstick frying pan or 2 smaller pans over medium-high heat, melt the butter with the olive oil. Divide the potato mixture into 4 equal portions and place each portion in a free-form spoonful in the pan(s). Flatten each mound with a spatula, then cover and cook until browned on the bottom, 4–6 minutes. Turn the potatoes, flatten again and cook until browned and crisp on the second side, 4–6 minutes longer.

Serve immediately.

Serves 2–4

French Fries

The keys to crisp French fries are drying the potatoes well, using fresh oil, maintaining the oil at a constant high temperature, not crowding the potatoes in the pan and never covering the pan. The traditional method calls for cooking the potatoes twice. The first immersion in oil cooks the centers of the fries and firms their exteriors. The second cooking makes the potatoes crisp and golden brown.

If you do not have a deep-fat fryer, use a deep, heavy saucepan and long-handled tongs or a wire skimmer. You will also need a deep-fat frying thermometer if the fryer lacks a built-in thermostat or if using a saucepan.

While the following method recommends peeling the potatoes, you may prefer to leave the skins on for a more rustic presentation. Either way they're delicious.

There are a number of ways to cut the potatoes: try the French-fry attachment of a food processor, any of the French-fry cutting tools on the market, or a very sharp knife.

2 lb (1 kg) baking potatoes, each about 4 inches
  (10 cm) long
vegetable oil, for deep-frying
salt

Peel the potatoes and cut them lengthwise into slices ⅜ inch (9 mm) thick. Then cut each slice lengthwise into strips ⅜ inch (9 mm) wide. Place in a bowl, add water to cover and let stand for 5 minutes to remove excess starch.

Meanwhile, pour oil to a depth of 2 inches (5 cm) into a deep-fat fryer with a basket or into a deep, heavy pan. Heat to 330°F (170°C), checking the temperature on a built-in thermostat or a deep-fat thermometer. If you do not have a thermometer, drop in a piece of potato; the oil should immediately begin to foam along its edges.

While the oil is heating, line platters or trays with paper towels. Thoroughly dry the potatoes with kitchen towels. (Wet potatoes may stick together and will cause the oil to splatter.) If using a fryer, briefly immerse the basket in the hot oil to prevent the potatoes from sticking to it once they are added. Remove the basket

from the oil, place 2 handfuls of the potatoes in the basket and lower into the oil. Alternatively, carefully lower them in the pan of oil using a skimmer or tongs. The oil will expand and cover the potatoes. Be sure not to add too many potatoes at one time or they will not cook evenly. Fry until the potatoes are pale yellow but have not started to brown, 4–5 minutes. Remove the basket and rest over a bowl to drain, then transfer the French fries to paper towel–lined trays or platters for at least 10 minutes or for up to 2 hours. If removing with a skimmer or tongs, place directly on lined trays.

1. Cutting the fries.
With a long, sharp knife, cut peeled potatoes lengthwise into slices of desired thickness. Then cut each slice lengthwise into even strips.

2. Soaking in water.
To remove excess surface starch, soak the potatoes in water to cover for 5 minutes while the oil is heating. Drain and dry the potatoes thoroughly using kitchen towels.

3. Testing oil temperature.
The oil is ready for frying when it reaches 330°F (170°C) on a deep-fat frying thermometer. Or test it with a piece of potato, which should foam on contact.

Just before serving, line additional trays or platters with paper towels. Reheat the oil to 370°F (188°C) and fry the potatoes again in batches until golden brown and crisp, 3–5 minutes. Remove the basket and drain over a bowl and then turn them out onto the lined trays. Or remove with a skimmer, draining well over the pan, and transfer to lined trays.

Place in a serving bowl or basket, season to taste with salt and serve immediately.

Serves 4

4. Precooking the potatoes.
Place a small batch of potatoes in the frying basket or pan and fry just until pale yellow, 4–5 minutes, to cook their centers and firm them up. Remove from the oil and set aside on paper towels to drain.

5. Crisping the potatoes.
Raise the oil's temperature to 370°F (188°C). Return the potatoes to the oil and fry until golden brown and crisp, 3–5 minutes longer.

6. Draining the fries.
Drain the oil from the basket, then spread the fries on a tray lined with paper towels to soak up excess oil. Serve hot, sprinkled to taste with salt or other seasonings.

FRIES OF ALL SHAPES AND SIZES

Shoestring Potatoes. Unlike French fries, shoestring potatoes are cooked only once. Peel the potatoes and cut them lengthwise into slices ¼ inch (6 mm) thick. Then cut each slice lengthwise into strips ¼ inch (6 mm) wide. Place in a bowl, add water to cover and let stand for 5 minutes to remove excess starch. Meanwhile, pour oil to a depth of 2 inches (5 cm) into a deep-fat fryer or deep, heavy saucepan. Heat the oil to 375°F (190°C). While the oil is heating, thoroughly dry the potatoes with kitchen towels, then cook in batches as directed for French fries, stirring with long tongs to prevent the potatoes from sticking together, until golden brown, 8–10 minutes.

Potato Chips. Potato chips (known in Britain as "crisps") must be cooked in smaller batches than French fries are, to ensure crisp, golden brown results. Peel the potatoes and cut into slices ¹⁄₁₆ inch (2 mm) thick. Place in a bowl, add water to cover and let stand for 5 minutes to remove excess starch. Drain the potatoes and dry thoroughly. Fry as directed for French fries, but cook only 1 handful of potatoes at a time and allow only about 3 minutes for the first cooking and 3–4 minutes for the second cooking.

Roasted Cajun Potatoes

2½ lb (1.25 kg) yellow-fleshed, red or
   white potatoes (5 or 6 potatoes)
¼ cup (2 fl oz/60 ml) vegetable oil or
   olive oil
2 shallots, finely chopped
1 clove garlic, minced
1 teaspoon salt
½ teaspoon paprika
½ teaspoon cayenne pepper
½ teaspoon freshly ground black pepper
2 tablespoons chopped fresh parsley,
   optional

Cajun spices add a lively spark to simple roasted potatoes. Serve these spiced-up favorites with a simple main course of grilled pork chops or chicken. Flavorful yellow-fleshed potatoes are a particularly good variety to use for this dish.

❧

*P*reheat an oven to 450°F (230°C).

Peel the potatoes, then rinse under cold running water and pat dry with a kitchen towel. Cut each potato lengthwise into 8 wedges.

In a roasting pan stir together the oil, shallots, garlic, salt, paprika, cayenne pepper and black pepper. Add the potatoes and, using a large spoon or by shaking the pan from side to side, coat them evenly with the oil mixture.

Roast the potatoes, turning them every 15 minutes, until tender and golden brown, about 45 minutes. Taste and adjust the seasoning.

Transfer to a serving dish, garnish with the parsley if desired and serve immediately.

Serves 4–6

Roasted New Potatoes with Red Onions

2 lb (1 kg) small new red potatoes, unpeeled

2 tablespoons olive oil

1 teaspoon salt

¼ teaspoon freshly ground pepper

1 large red (Spanish) onion, coarsely chopped

¾ cup (6 fl oz/180 ml) chicken stock

2 tablespoons chopped fresh parsley

Roasted onion adds a delicious caramelized crispness to this side dish. If you can't find small new potatoes, cut more mature potatoes into 1½-inch (4-cm) pieces. Serve with frittatas, omelets or scrambled eggs.

Preheat an oven to 425°F (220°C).

Scrub the potatoes under cold running water and pat dry with a kitchen towel. In a roasting pan combine the potatoes, olive oil, salt and pepper. Using a large spoon or by shaking the pan from side to side, coat the potatoes evenly with the oil mixture.

Roast the potatoes for 20 minutes. Sprinkle evenly with the onion and drizzle evenly with the chicken stock. Continue roasting, shaking the pan every 10–15 minutes to rotate the potatoes, until they are brown and crusty and the onions are caramelized, 1–1¼ hours longer. Taste and adjust the seasoning.

Transfer to a serving bowl and garnish with the parsley. Serve immediately.

Serves 4–6

Baked Potato Crisps

2 baking potatoes, ½–¾ lb (250–375 g)
  each, unpeeled and well scrubbed
1 tablespoon olive oil or olive oil cooking
  spray
salt
freshly ground pepper
1 teaspoon chopped fresh chives,
  optional
1 teaspoon chopped fresh parsley,
  optional

These light, crisp chips take only a little time to prepare. Use olive oil cooking spray, if available, to moisten the potatoes lightly. Substitute a sprinkling of your favorite herbs for the chives and parsley, and add a dusting of cayenne pepper and paprika or Parmesan cheese with the herbs, if you like.

*P*reheat an oven to 400°F (200°C). Oil 2 nonstick baking sheets with olive oil.

Cut the potatoes into slices ⅛ inch (3 mm) thick. Place the potatoes in a bowl and toss with the olive oil to coat evenly, or coat with the spray. Season to taste with salt and pepper.

Place on the prepared baking sheets. Bake until crisp and browned, 20–25 minutes.

Transfer to a serving dish and toss with the chives and parsley if desired. Taste and adjust the seasoning. Serve immediately.

Serves 2–4

Roasted New Potatoes with Lemon, Basil and Chives

2½ lb (1.25 kg) new red or white
   potatoes, unpeeled
¼ cup (2 fl oz/60 ml) olive oil
2 tablespoons fresh lemon juice
1 teaspoon salt
¼ teaspoon paprika
½ teaspoon freshly ground pepper
1 tablespoon finely chopped fresh basil
1 tablespoon finely chopped fresh chives

Simple seasonings coat these crisp, golden brown potatoes, making them a good accompaniment to scrambled eggs, roasted chicken or lamb chops.

Preheat an oven to 425°F (220°C).

Wash the potatoes under cold running water and pat dry with a kitchen towel.

In a roasting pan stir together the olive oil, lemon juice, salt, paprika and pepper. Add the potatoes and, using a large spoon or by shaking the pan from side to side, coat the potatoes evenly with the oil mixture.

Roast the potatoes, turning every 15 minutes, until tender and golden brown, about 45 minutes. Taste and adjust the seasoning.

Transfer to a serving dish and garnish with the basil and chives. Serve immediately.

Serves 4–6

Potato Chili Gratin

4 fresh Anaheim or poblano chili
  peppers
1 tablespoon vegetable oil
1 clove garlic, minced
2½ lb (1.25 kg) red potatoes, peeled and
  cut into slices ⅛ inch (3 mm) thick
  or thinner
1¼ cups (10 fl oz/310 ml) milk
1 cup (8 fl oz/250 ml) heavy (double)
  cream
1 teaspoon salt
⅛ teaspoon freshly ground pepper
1 cup (4 oz/125 g) shredded Gruyère
  cheese
3 tablespoons fine dried bread crumbs

Serve as a first course in individual gratin dishes or as an accompaniment to any simple meat dish. If you like, sauté some extra chilies to use as a garnish.

Roast and peel the chilies (see glossary, page 106), then seed, derib and cut into ¼-inch (6-mm) dice. Leave the broiler on.

In a frying pan over medium heat, warm the oil. Add the diced chilies and sauté until slightly softened, 3–5 minutes. Add the garlic and sauté for 1 minute longer. Set aside.

Place the potato slices in a kitchen towel and wring out all moisture. Pour the milk into a large, deep, heavy saucepan and place over medium heat. Drop in the potatoes, separating the slices as you do, and bring to a boil. Reduce the heat to low, cover and simmer, stirring occasionally, for 10 minutes. Uncover and simmer until most of the milk has been absorbed, 3–5 minutes longer; do not scorch.

Add the cream, salt and pepper and return to a boil. Reduce the heat to low, cover and simmer, stirring occasionally, for 10 minutes. Uncover and simmer until nearly all the cream has been absorbed, 3–5 minutes longer; do not scorch. Taste and adjust the seasoning.

Butter a 9-inch (23-cm) flameproof baking dish with 2-inch (5-cm) sides. Transfer half of the potato mixture to the dish. Layer the chilies evenly on top. Cover with the remaining potatoes. Sprinkle with the cheese and then the bread crumbs. Slip the dish under the broiler 4 inches (10 cm) from the heat and broil (grill) until nicely browned, 8–10 minutes. Be careful, as the bread crumbs burn easily. Serve immediately.

Serves 4–6

Broccoli-and-Cheese-Stuffed Potatoes

salt to taste, plus ½ teaspoon salt
1 lb (500 g) broccoli, stems removed and
   florets cut into ½-inch (12-mm) pieces
4 basic baked potatoes, hot (recipe on
   page 9)
3 tablespoons unsalted butter
⅔ cup (5 fl oz/160 ml) milk, heated
1¼ cups (5 oz/155 g) shredded sharp
   Cheddar cheese
pinch of white pepper

If you cut the potatoes in half, you can serve the stuffed halves as a side dish for 8. This is also a wonderful luncheon main course with a crisp green salad.

Preheat an oven to 400°F (200°C).

Fill a saucepan three-fourths full with water and bring to a boil over high heat. Add salt to taste and the broccoli florets. Reduce the heat to medium, cover with the lid ajar and cook until tender, 5–7 minutes. Remove from the heat, drain well and let cool completely.

Meanwhile, using a sharp knife, cut out an oval of the skin on the top of each potato and remove it. Carefully scoop out all but a thin shell of the potato pulp. Alternatively, cut each potato in half and scoop out the potato pulp from each half, leaving only a thin shell. Pass the potato pulp through a potato ricer into a bowl, or place the pulp in a bowl and mash it with a potato masher. Add the butter, milk, 1 cup (4 oz/125 g) of the cheese, the ½ teaspoon salt and the white pepper. Stir vigorously to combine. Add the broccoli and mix gently until evenly incorporated. Adjust the seasoning.

Dividing the potato mixture evenly, spoon it back into the potato shells, mounding the tops attractively. Sprinkle the remaining cheese evenly over the tops. Place on an ungreased baking sheet and bake until the potatoes are hot throughout and the cheese has melted and is bubbling, 10–15 minutes. Serve immediately.

Serves 4 or 8

Mediterranean Potato Gratin

3 tablespoons olive oil

1 yellow onion, thinly sliced

1 red bell pepper (capsicum), seeded, deribbed and thinly sliced lengthwise

1 lb (500 g) tomatoes, peeled, seeded and chopped

2 cloves garlic, minced

¼ teaspoon red pepper flakes, optional

salt

freshly ground black pepper

4 tablespoons chopped fresh basil

2 lb (1 kg) baking potatoes, peeled and cut into slices ¼ inch (6 mm) thick

1 cup (4 oz/125 g) shredded Gruyère cheese

A zesty potato dish that makes a wonderful accompaniment to grilled lamb chops or roast leg of lamb. Or serve it as a vegetarian main course with a mixed green salad. If the bell pepper is quite long, cut it in half crosswise before slicing.

Preheat an oven to 400°F (200°C). Oil a 9-inch (23-cm) gratin dish with 2-inch (5-cm) sides.

In a large frying pan over medium heat, warm 2 tablespoons of the olive oil. Add the onion and sauté until soft but not browned, 3–5 minutes. Add the bell pepper and sauté for 3 minutes longer. Add the tomatoes and cook, stirring, for another 3 minutes. Raise the heat to high and cook, stirring, until the excess moisture from the tomatoes evaporates, 1–2 minutes. Add the garlic and cook for 1 minute longer. Add the pepper flakes, if desired, salt and pepper to taste and 2 tablespoons of the basil. Taste and adjust the seasoning.

Spread half of the potatoes on the bottom of the prepared dish. Arrange half of the vegetable mixture on top and sprinkle with half of the cheese. Repeat the layers. Drizzle the remaining 1 tablespoon oil evenly over the top. Cover tightly with aluminum foil.

Place the covered dish on a baking sheet. Bake for 30 minutes. Remove the foil and continue to bake until the potatoes are tender and the top is nicely browned, about 15 minutes longer. Sprinkle with the remaining 2 tablespoons basil and serve immediately.

Serves 4–6

Pesto-Baked Potato Wedges

2 basic baked potatoes, hot *(recipe on page 9)*
3 tablespoons pesto *(recipe on page 10)*

These tasty wedges are a pretty accompaniment to grilled chicken, fish or steak. Serve them bubbling hot.

*P*reheat a broiler (griller).

Cut each potato in half lengthwise and then in half again, to create 4 wedges. Spread the cut sides of each wedge evenly with some of the pesto and place the wedges on an ungreased baking sheet, pesto side up.

Place under the broiler and broil (grill) until bubbling, about 3 minutes. Serve immediately.

Serves 2–4

Parmesan-Roasted Potatoes

3 lb (1.5 kg) baking potatoes, unpeeled
   and well scrubbed
salt to taste, plus 1 teaspoon salt
3 tablespoons olive oil
¼ teaspoon freshly ground pepper
½ cup (2 oz/60 g) freshly shredded
   Parmesan cheese
2 tablespoons finely chopped fresh
   parsley

Although very little oil is used, these potatoes taste almost fried.
Be sure to buy high-quality Parmesan cheese for these crisp gems.
Serve them with grilled steaks, lamb chops or braised chicken.

*P*reheat an oven to 450°F (230°C). Oil a roasting pan with olive oil.

Cut each potato into 1½-inch (4-cm) cubes. Fill a large pot three-fourths full with water and bring to a boil over high heat. Add salt to taste and the potatoes and boil for 5 minutes. Drain well and pat dry with a kitchen towel.

In a large bowl stir together the olive oil, the 1 teaspoon salt and the pepper. Add the potato cubes and toss to coat evenly.

Spread the potatoes in the prepared pan. Roast, turning every few minutes to prevent sticking, until tender and golden brown, 20–25 minutes. Taste and adjust the seasoning.

Transfer to a serving dish. Add the Parmesan cheese and parsley and toss to coat evenly. Serve immediately.

Serves 4

Baked Yams with Tomatillo Sour Cream

4 uniformly sized and shaped yam-type
   sweet potatoes, ½–¾ lb (250–375 g)
   each, unpeeled and well scrubbed
2 teaspoons vegetable oil
½ cup (4 fl oz/125 ml) sour cream
1–2 tablespoons commercial green
   tomatillo salsa
1 teaspoon fresh lime juice
salt
freshly ground pepper
1 tablespoon finely chopped fresh
   cilantro (fresh coriander)

The spicy tomatillo cream heightens the mellow flavor of the yam-type sweet potatoes. These are especially good served with grilled chicken breasts that have been prepared in a citrus marinade.

Preheat an oven to 400°F (200°C). Rub the potatoes all over with the oil and place on an ungreased baking sheet in the middle of the oven. Bake for 30 minutes. Prick the skin in a few places with a fork and continue to bake until tender when pierced with a fork, about 30 minutes longer.

While the potatoes are baking, in a small bowl stir together the sour cream, salsa, lime juice and salt and pepper to taste. Taste and adjust the seasoning.

When the potatoes are done, transfer to individual plates. Using a sharp knife split each potato open lengthwise, cutting only halfway through. Spoon a few tablespoons of the sour cream mixture into each potato and then garnish with the cilantro. Serve immediately.

Serves 4

Ratatouille-Stuffed New Potatoes

FOR THE POTATOES:

1½ lb (750 g) small new red potatoes,
   12–16, unpeeled and well scrubbed
2 tablespoons olive oil

FOR THE FILLING:

2 tablespoons olive oil
1 small yellow onion, finely chopped
1 globe eggplant (aubergine), 1½–2 lb
   (750 g–1 kg), peeled and cut into
   ⅛-inch (3-mm) dice
2 red bell peppers (capsicums), seeded,
   deribbed and cut into ⅛-inch (3-mm)
   dice
2 lb (1 kg) plum (Roma) tomatoes,
   peeled, seeded and finely chopped
2 cloves garlic, minced
2 tablespoons finely chopped fresh basil
1 tablespoon balsamic vinegar
1 teaspoon salt
¼ teaspoon freshly ground pepper

½ cup (2 oz/60 g) freshly grated
   Parmesan cheese

Tiny new potatoes make great appetizers because they are easy to pick up. These luscious stuffed potatoes are also a fine side dish to grilled sea bass or halibut.

*P*reheat an oven to 475°F (240°C). Place the potatoes on a baking sheet in the middle of the oven. Bake until tender and slightly crispy, 45–50 minutes; test with a knife or skewer. Remove and let cool. Leave the oven set at 475°F (240°C).

   Cut each potato in half crosswise. If the ends are uneven, cut off a thin slice so they will stand upright once filled. Scoop out the pulp from each half, leaving only a thin shell of pulp; reserve the pulp for another use. Return the potato shells to the baking sheet, hollow sides down, and brush the skins with olive oil. Bake until crisp, 10–15 minutes. Remove from the oven and reduce the oven temperature to 425°F (220°C).

   Meanwhile, make the filling: In a large frying pan over medium heat, warm the olive oil. Add the onion and sauté, stirring frequently, until translucent, about 5 minutes. Add the eggplant and cook, stirring, until beginning to soften, 5–7 minutes. Add the bell peppers and cook, stirring, 5 minutes longer. Add the tomatoes, garlic, basil and vinegar and continue cooking until the liquid evaporates and the eggplant is soft, 5–10 minutes longer. Season with the salt and pepper. Set aside.

   Sprinkle the inside of the potato shells with some of the Parmesan cheese. Spoon in the filling and place on an ungreased baking sheet. Sprinkle with the remaining cheese. Bake until heated through, 10–15 minutes. Serve immediately.

Serves 10–12 as an appetizer, 6–8 as a side dish

Stuffed Potatoes with Red Pepper Aïoli

4 basic baked potatoes, hot *(recipe on page 9)*

⅔ cup (5 fl oz/160 ml) milk, heated

¾ cup (6 fl oz/180 ml) red pepper aïoli *(recipe on page 11)*

5 tablespoons freshly grated Parmesan cheese

½ teaspoon salt

pinch of white pepper

2 tablespoons chopped fresh parsley

A garlicky roasted pepper mayonnaise gives a Mediterranean accent to these stuffed baked potatoes. They are delicious with herb-roasted meats, poultry or fish.

Preheat an oven to 400°F (200°C).

Using a sharp knife, cut out an oval of the skin on the top of each potato and remove it. Carefully scoop out all but a thin shell of the potato pulp. Alternatively, cut each potato in half and scoop out the potato pulp from each half, leaving only a thin shell. Pass the potato pulp through a potato ricer into a bowl, or place the pulp in a bowl and mash it with a potato masher. Add the milk, ½ cup (4 fl oz/125 ml) of the aïoli, 3 tablespoons of the cheese, salt and white pepper. Stir vigorously to combine. Taste and adjust the seasoning.

Dividing the potato mixture evenly, spoon it back into the potato shells, mounding the tops attractively. Sprinkle the remaining 2 tablespoons cheese evenly over the tops of the potatoes.

Place the stuffed potatoes on a baking sheet. Bake until the potatoes are hot throughout and the cheese has melted and is bubbling, 10–15 minutes. Garnish with the remaining ¼ cup (2 fl oz/55 ml) aïoli and the parsley. Serve immediately.

Serves 4 or 8

Potatoes Dauphinois

1 tablespoon unsalted butter, melted

2 lb (1 kg) baking potatoes, peeled and cut into slices ¼ inch (6 mm) thick

2 cloves garlic, minced

1 cup (4 oz/125 g) shredded Gruyère cheese

1 cup (8 fl oz/250 ml) half-and-half

salt

white pepper

There are many different versions of this potato dish, which originates in the Dauphiné region of southeast France. One version includes a rich egg custard poured over the potatoes, which are then sprinkled with grated cheese. In this interpretation, eggs are omitted, but a creamier consistency is possible by substituting crème fraîche or heavy (double) cream for the half-and-half. An extra bonus is that these luscious potatoes reheat beautifully in a 350°F (180°C) oven.

Preheat an oven to 350°F (180°C).

Brush a 9-inch (23-cm) gratin dish with 2-inch (5-cm) sides with the melted butter. Layer half of the potatoes in the dish. Sprinkle with all of the garlic and half of the cheese. Pour ½ cup (4 fl oz/125 ml) of the half-and-half evenly over the top. Sprinkle lightly with salt to taste and a pinch of white pepper. Layer the remaining potatoes on top and then top with the remaining cheese. Sprinkle lightly with salt to taste and a pinch of white pepper. Pour the remaining ½ cup (4 fl oz/125 ml) half-and-half evenly over the top.

Place the gratin dish on a baking sheet. Bake until the top is golden brown and the potatoes are tender, about 1 hour. Serve immediately.

Serves 4

Mexican Crispy Baked Potato Skins

4 basic baked potatoes, hot *(recipe on page 9)*

2 tablespoons olive oil

1 cup (4 oz/125 g) shredded Monterey jack or sharp Cheddar cheese, or half of each

½ cup (4 fl oz/125 ml) spicy tomato salsa *(recipe on page 11)*

½ cup (4 fl oz/125 ml) sour cream

Brushing potato skins with oil provides extra crispness. These are tasty appetizers to serve with a pitcher of frosty margaritas. Follow with chicken tostadas or carne asada—*beef marinated in lime juice and onion and then grilled.*

*P*reheat an oven to 450°F (220°C).

Split each potato in half lengthwise. Using a spoon scoop out the potato pulp from each half, leaving shells ½ inch (12 mm) thick. Use the potato pulp for mashed potatoes or another use. Cut the skins into wedge shapes.

Brush the skin side of each piece with a light coating of olive oil. Place the potatoes, skin sides down, on an ungreased baking sheet. Sprinkle the cheese evenly over the tops. Bake until the cheese melts, about 10 minutes.

Transfer to a serving platter and garnish with the salsa and sour cream. Serve immediately.

Serves 4–6

42

Potatoes Savoyarde

1 tablespoon unsalted butter, melted,
plus 3 tablespoons unsalted butter, cut
into small pieces
3 cloves garlic, minced
2 tablespoons finely chopped fresh
parsley
1½ cups (6 oz/185 g) shredded Gruyère
cheese
¼ teaspoon freshly ground pepper
2½ lb (1.25 kg) baking potatoes,
unpeeled and well scrubbed, cut into
slices ¼ inch (6 mm) thick
1½ cups (12 fl oz/375 ml) chicken or
beef stock

*This crusty potato gratin from Savoy, a mountainous region of
southeast France, uses chicken or beef stock and a bit of butter to
moisten and flavor the potatoes. Serve with roast beef, grilled
steaks or barbecued chicken.*

Preheat an oven to 375°F (190°C). Brush a 2-qt (2-l) baking
dish (a soufflé dish works well) with the melted butter.

In a small bowl stir together the garlic, parsley, cheese and
pepper.

Layer one-third of the potatoes in the prepared dish and
sprinkle one-third of the garlic-cheese mixture over the top.
Dot with 1 tablespoon of the butter pieces. Repeat the layers
once and then top with the remaining potatoes. Pour the
stock evenly over the layers. Sprinkle the remaining garlic-
cheese mixture evenly over the top and dot with the
remaining butter pieces. Butter a piece of aluminum foil on
one side large enough to cover the dish. Place it over the
dish, buttered side down.

Bake for 30 minutes. Remove the foil and continue baking
until the potatoes are tender and the top is brown and
crusty, 30–40 minutes longer. Serve immediately.

Serves 6

Baked Sweet Potatoes with Crème Fraîche and Onions

2 uniformly sized and shaped sweet
   potatoes, ½–¾ lb (250–375 g) each,
   unpeeled and well scrubbed
2 teaspoons vegetable oil
¼ cup (2 fl oz/60 ml) crème fraîche
1 tablespoon finely chopped green
   (spring) onion, including green tops

This is a winning last-minute dish. The potatoes look pretty contrasted with the white of the crème fraîche and the green of the onions. Sour cream can be substituted for the crème fraîche.

Preheat an oven to 400°F (200°C).

   Rub the sweet potatoes all over with the oil and place on an ungreased baking sheet. Bake for 30 minutes. Prick the skin in a few places with fork tines and continue to bake until tender when pierced with a fork, about 30 minutes longer.

   Cut off the ends of the hot sweet potatoes and peel the potatoes if desired. Cut crosswise into slices 1½ inches (4 cm) thick. Arrange a few slices, overlapping or next to one another, on each individual plate. Or spoon the potatoes into a serving bowl. Garnish with the crème fraîche and green onion. Serve immediately.

Serves 4–6

Cheese-Stuffed Baked Potatoes

4 basic baked potatoes, hot (*recipe on
    page 9*)
3 tablespoons unsalted butter
⅔ cup (5 fl oz/160 ml) milk, heated
¾ cup (3 oz/90 g) plus 2 tablespoons
    shredded Fontina cheese
3 tablespoons plus 2 teaspoons freshly
    grated Parmesan cheese
½ teaspoon salt
pinch of white pepper

*These stuffed potatoes are an excellent accompaniment to steak or
roast beef. Feel free to use other cheeses. Fontina is a mild cheese;
Gruyère is a good substitute. You can reserve the oval potato-skin
tops, sprinkle them with cheese or spread them with pesto (recipe
on page 10) and rebake with the stuffed potatoes.*

Preheat an oven to 400°F (200°C).

Using a sharp knife, cut out an oval of the skin on the top
of each potato and remove it. Carefully scoop out all but a
thin shell of the potato pulp. Alternatively, cut each potato
in half and scoop out the potato pulp from each half, leaving
only a thin shell.

Pass the potato pulp through a potato ricer into a bowl, or
place the pulp in a bowl and mash it with a potato masher.
Add the butter, milk, the ¾ cup (3 oz/90 g) Fontina, the
3 tablespoons Parmesan, salt and white pepper. Stir
vigorously to combine. Taste and adjust the seasoning.

Dividing the potato mixture evenly, spoon it back into the
potato shells, mounding the tops attractively. Sprinkle the
2 tablespoons Fontina and 2 teaspoons Parmesan evenly
over the tops of the potatoes.

Place the stuffed potatoes on an ungreased baking sheet.
Bake until the potatoes are hot throughout and the cheese
has melted and is bubbling, 10–15 minutes. Serve
immediately.

Serves 4 or 8

Rum-Glazed Candied Yams

4 uniformly sized yam-type sweet
  potatoes, about ½ lb (250 g) each,
  unpeeled and well scrubbed

FOR THE GLAZE:
¾ cup (6 oz/185 g) firmly packed dark
  brown sugar
6 tablespoons (3 fl oz/90 ml) light rum
¼ cup (2 oz/60 g) unsalted butter
⅛ teaspoon ground cinnamon
⅛ teaspoon ground allspice
⅛ teaspoon ground nutmeg
⅛ teaspoon ground ginger

fresh mint leaves, for garnish

*Rum adds a slightly exotic touch to the caramel-spiced glaze that
tops this holiday-time American favorite. Two methods are given
for finishing the dish, depending upon whether you are short of
oven or stove-top space. You can use ½ teaspoon pumpkin pie
spice in place of the assorted spices.*

*F*ill a large pot three-fourths full with water and bring to a
boil. Add the potatoes and simmer until tender but slightly
resistant when pierced with a fork, 35–45 minutes. Drain
and let cool. Peel the potatoes and slice off the ends. Then
cut crosswise into slices about 2 inches (5 cm) thick.

  If baking the potatoes, preheat an oven to 400°F (200°C).
Butter a large 9-inch (23-cm) baking dish and arrange the
potatoes, cut sides down, in it. To make the glaze, in a
saucepan over medium heat, combine the sugar, rum, butter
and spices. Simmer, stirring, until the sugar dissolves and
the syrup is slightly thickened, about 3 minutes. Pour evenly
over the potatoes. Place the dish in the middle of the oven
and bake, basting about every 5 minutes, until a glaze forms
on top, about 15 minutes. Garnish with mint leaves. Serve
immediately, directly from the dish.

  Alternatively, if cooking on the stove top, combine the
glaze ingredients in a large, heavy pot over medium heat.
Simmer, stirring, until the sugar dissolves and the syrup is
slightly thickened, about 3 minutes. Add the potatoes and
simmer gently, basting frequently, until the potatoes are
nicely glazed, 10–15 minutes. Arrange on a platter or place
in a bowl and garnish with mint leaves.

Serves 6–8

Scalloped Potatoes

1 tablespoon unsalted butter, melted,
  plus 3 tablespoons unsalted butter, cut
  into small pieces
1 clove garlic, minced
3 tablespoons all-purpose (plain) flour
1½ teaspoons salt
⅛ teaspoon white pepper
3 lb (1.5 kg) yellow-fleshed or white
  potatoes, peeled and sliced ¼ inch
  (6 mm) thick
1 small onion, thinly sliced
3 cups (24 fl oz/750 ml) milk
2 tablespoons finely chopped fresh
  parsley

*In this classic dish, potatoes bake in a flour-and-milk mixture
that forms a creamy sauce. The onion layers provide a sweet
undertone. If you prefer an even creamier result, use baking
potatoes, which take on a softer texture during cooking. Serve
with any simple roast meat or chicken dish.*

Preheat an oven to 350°F (180°C). Brush a 9- by 13-inch
(23- by 33-cm) baking dish with the melted butter.

In a small bowl stir together the garlic, flour, salt and
white pepper.

Arrange one-third of the potatoes in the bottom of the
prepared dish and top with one-half of the onion slices.
Sprinkle half of the flour mixture over the onion and dot
with 1 tablespoon of the butter pieces. Repeat the layers and
dot again with 1 tablespoon of the butter pieces. Layer with
the remaining potatoes and dot with the remaining butter
pieces. Pour the milk evenly over the top. Butter a piece of
aluminum foil on one side large enough to cover the dish.
Place it over the dish, buttered side down.

Place the covered dish on a baking sheet and place in the
middle of the oven. Bake for 50 minutes. Remove the foil
and continue baking until the top is golden brown and the
potatoes are tender, about 45 minutes longer.

Sprinkle with the parsley and serve immediately.

Serves 6–8

New Potatoes with Caviar

1½ lb (750 g) small new red potatoes,
   12–16, unpeeled and well scrubbed
2 tablespoons vegetable oil
¾ cup (6 fl oz/180 ml) sour cream or
   crème fraîche
2 teaspoons finely chopped fresh chives
¼ teaspoon salt
pinch of white pepper
2 oz (60 g) any variety fish roe or caviar
watercress or fresh parsley sprigs

For an attractive presentation use golden caviar, salmon roe and, of course—if you can afford it—the real thing.

Preheat an oven to 475°F (240°C).

Place the potatoes on an ungreased baking sheet. Bake until cooked through and slightly crispy, 45–50 minutes; prick with a knife or skewer to test for doneness. Remove from the oven and let cool. Cut each potato in half crosswise. If the ends of any potatoes are uneven, cut off a thin slice from them, so they will stand upright once they are filled. Carefully scoop out all the pulp from each half, leaving only a thin shell. Place the pulp in a bowl. Return the potato shells to the baking sheet, hollow sides down, and brush the skins with the oil. Return to the oven and bake until crisp, 10–15 minutes. Remove from the oven and reduce the temperature to 425°F (220°C).

To the potato pulp add ½ cup (4 fl oz/125 ml) of the sour cream or crème fraîche, the chives, salt and white pepper and mix well. Pack the potato mixture into a pastry bag fitted with a medium star tip and pipe the potato mixture into the shells. Alternatively, using a small teaspoon, spoon the mixture into the shells.

Place the filled potatoes on an ungreased baking sheet. Bake until heated through, 10–15 minutes. Arrange the potatoes on a round serving platter. Garnish each with a dollop of the remaining sour cream or crème fraîche, then of caviar. Garnish the platter with watercress or parsley sprigs and serve immediately.

Serves 10–12 as an appetizer

Yam Soufflé with Pecan Topping

FOR THE TOPPING:

½ cup (2 oz/60 g) coarsely chopped
   pecans
10 gingersnap cookies, coarsely chopped
¼ cup (2 oz/60 g) firmly packed dark
   brown sugar

FOR THE SOUFFLÉ:

4 yam-type sweet potatoes, about ½ lb
   (250 g) each, unpeeled and well
   scrubbed
½ cup (4 fl oz/125 ml) half-and-half
2 tablespoons unsalted butter, melted
½ cup (4 fl oz/125 ml) freshly squeezed
   orange juice
3 tablespoons firmly packed dark brown
   sugar
3 tablespoons orange marmalade
½ teaspoon ground cinnamon
½ teaspoon ground ginger
½ teaspoon ground allspice
¼ teaspoon ground nutmeg
4 egg yolks
5 egg whites
¼ teaspoon salt
¼ teaspoon cream of tartar

2 tablespoons unsalted butter, cut into
   small pieces

To make this rich soufflé, choose the reddish yam-type sweet potato for its creamy flesh. If you like, use 1¾ teaspoons pumpkin pie spice in place of the cinnamon, ginger, allspice and nutmeg.

To make the topping, preheat an oven to 350°F (180°C). Place the pecans on a baking sheet and toast in the oven until brown, 5–7 minutes. Transfer to a bowl, add the gingersnaps and sugar and stir to mix. Set aside.

Raise the oven temperature to 400°F (200°C). To make the soufflé, butter a deep 2-qt (2-l) baking dish or soufflé dish. Wrap each yam in aluminum foil and place on a baking sheet in the middle of the oven. Bake until very soft when pierced, 45–60 minutes. Remove from the oven and let cool. Reduce the oven temperature to 350°F (180°C).

Scoop the pulp from the potatoes and measure out 4 cups (2 lb/1 kg). Place in a bowl and add the half-and-half, melted butter, orange juice, sugar, marmalade and spices. Using an electric mixer set on low speed, beat until combined. Taste and adjust with more spice. Add the egg yolks, one at a time, beating well after each addition.

In a large bowl and using an electric mixer with clean beaters, beat the egg whites until foamy. Add the salt and cream of tartar and continue beating until stiff peaks form. Gently fold the egg whites into the potato mixture until no white streaks remain. Spoon into the prepared dish. Sprinkle evenly with the topping. Dot with the butter pieces. Bake until puffed and browned, 1–1¼ hours. If the topping begins to brown too much, cover loosely with aluminum foil. Serve immediately.

Serves 8–10

Cheese Potato Gratin

1 tablespoon unsalted butter, melted,
  plus 1 tablespoon unsalted butter, at
  room temperature, cut into small
  pieces
2 cloves garlic, minced
2 tablespoons finely chopped fresh basil
1 teaspoon finely chopped fresh thyme
¼ teaspoon salt
⅛ teaspoon white pepper
1 cup (4 oz/125 g) crumbled Gorgonzola
3 lb (1.5 kg) white, red, yellow-fleshed
  or baking potatoes, peeled and cut into
  slices ¼ inch (6 mm) thick
1½ cups (12 fl oz/375 ml) half-and-half
2 tablespoons chopped fresh parsley

Here, potatoes are mixed with tangy Gorgonzola cheese and herbs. There are a number of types of Gorgonzola, known to be Italy's oldest blue. If you prefer a milder flavor, look for dolcelatte, also called sweet Gorgonzola, which is aged for less time than the more common variety.

*P*reheat an oven to 375°F (190°C). Brush a 10-inch (25-cm) baking dish with 2-inch (5-cm) sides with the melted butter.

In a small bowl stir together the garlic, basil, thyme, salt, white pepper and Gorgonzola.

Layer one-third of the potatoes in the bottom of the prepared dish. Sprinkle one-third of the herb-cheese mixture over the top. Repeat the layers once and then top with the remaining potatoes. Pour the half-and-half evenly over the potatoes and sprinkle the remaining herb-cheese mixture evenly over the top. Dot with the butter pieces. Butter a piece of aluminum foil large enough to cover the dish and place it, buttered side down, on the dish.

Bake for 30 minutes. Remove the foil and continue to bake until the top is brown and crusty and the potatoes are tender when pierced with a fork, 30–40 minutes longer. During the last 30–40 minutes of baking, baste occasionally with the liquid that forms in the dish from the half-and-half and cheese. (Doing this will make the top potatoes softer.) Sprinkle with the parsley and serve immediately.

Serves 6–8

Sweet Potatoes Anna

2½ lb (1.25 kg) sweet potatoes, peeled and sliced ⅛ inch (3 mm) thick
1½ cups (¾ lb/375 g) clarified unsalted butter, melted (*see glossary, page 104*)
salt
freshly ground pepper
2 tablespoons finely chopped fresh parsley

This elegant potato dish was created for and dedicated to a stylish French woman named Anna Deslions at the time of the Second Empire. Traditionally French cooks prepare it in a specially designed round two-handled copper casserole. For this version, any heavy round pan will suffice. Make sure to use clarified butter to prevent burning.

Preheat an oven to 400°F (200°C). Butter a 9-inch (23-cm) straight-sided, nonstick cake pan or ovenproof frying pan.

Starting at the center of the pan and forming concentric circles, cover the bottom with a layer of sweet potatoes, overlapping the slices. Drizzle with some of the melted butter and sprinkle with salt and pepper. Continue layering in this same manner until all the potatoes have been used.

Butter one side of a piece of aluminum foil large enough to cover the pan, then cover the pan, buttered side down. Place a heavy lid (smaller than the pan) on top to weight down the potato layers. Bake for 40 minutes. Remove the lid and foil and continue to bake until the potatoes are tender and the top is golden, about 20 minutes longer; do not overcook.

Let cool for 10 minutes. Using a narrow spatula, loosen the potatoes from the pan bottom. Invert a flat round platter over the pan and, holding the platter firmly in place, invert the pan, then lift it off; excess butter will flow onto the platter as well. To remove the excess butter, tilt the platter and pour it off.

Garnish with the parsley and cut into wedges to serve.

Serves 8

Mini Potato Pancakes with Smoked Salmon

1 small yellow onion, grated
2 baking potatoes, about ½ lb (250 g)
  each, peeled and shredded
2 eggs
½ teaspoon salt
pinch of freshly ground pepper
2 tablespoons all-purpose (plain) flour
vegetable oil, for frying
⅓ cup (3 fl oz/80 ml) sour cream
4 tablespoons chopped smoked salmon
fresh dill sprigs

A lovely hors d'oeuvre or first course. Smoked trout or caviar is also an option here. Make these pancakes just before serving; they lose their crispness quickly. Excellent with your favorite sparkling wine.

Place the onion in a sieve and use a wooden spoon to press out all excess liquid. Transfer to a bowl. Press the excess liquid from the potatoes in the same way and add them to the onion. Add the eggs, salt, pepper and flour and, using the spoon, beat until the consistency of a thick batter.

Preheat an oven to 300°F (150°C). Line a large baking sheet with a double layer of paper towels. Pour oil to a depth of ½ inch (12 mm) into a large nonstick frying pan over medium-high heat. Spoon a rounded ½ tablespoon of batter into the pan to test the oil; the batter should hold together and begin to brown. When the oil is hot enough, working in batches, spoon rounded ½ tablespoons of the batter into the pan; make sure the pancakes do not touch. Flatten the pancakes with the back of a spoon; they should be about 1½ inches (4 cm) in diameter. Use a spatula to round and smooth the sides, if necessary. Fry until golden brown on the first side, 2–3 minutes. Flip and fry on the second side until golden brown, about 2 minutes longer.

Transfer the pancakes to the lined baking sheet to drain and place in the oven until all are cooked. Arrange the pancakes on a warmed serving platter. Garnish each with sour cream, smoked salmon and a dill sprig. Serve immediately.

Makes 30–36 pancakes; serves 8–12 as an appetizer

salt to taste, plus ½ teaspoon salt

2½ lb (1.25 kg) white potatoes, peeled and cut into ½-inch (12-mm) cubes

3 tablespoons unsalted butter

1 yellow onion, finely chopped

¼ cup (2 fl oz/60 ml) heavy (double) cream

4 tablespoons finely chopped fresh dill

pinch of white pepper

2 tablespoons vegetable oil

¼ lb (125 g) smoked salmon, coarsely chopped, plus 1 oz (30 g), cut into long, thin strips

Smoked Salmon Hash

Ask for less-expensive smoked salmon trimmings, since you'll need to chop the salmon anyway. This is a wonderful dish for Sunday brunch, accompanied with herbed scrambled eggs. Or serve it as a first course, presented in individual ramekins and garnished with a dollop of crème fraîche and a sprig of fresh dill.

Fill a large pot three-fourths full with water and bring to a boil. Add salt to taste and the potatoes and boil until not quite tender, 7–10 minutes. Drain well in a colander.

In a large nonstick frying pan over medium heat, melt 1 tablespoon of the butter. Add the onion and sauté until soft and translucent, 5–7 minutes. Transfer to a bowl and add the cooked potatoes, cream, 2 tablespoons of the dill, the ½ teaspoon salt and the white pepper. Stir well to combine.

Melt the remaining 2 tablespoons butter with the oil in the same frying pan over medium heat. Add the potato mixture and flatten firmly with a spatula. Cook until a crust forms on the underside, 5–7 minutes. Occasionally run the spatula around the edges of the potato mixture to keep it from sticking. Turn over and continue cooking, stirring frequently, until nicely cooked, 15–20 minutes longer. Be patient; the potatoes will brown slowly.

Add the chopped smoked salmon and mix just until thoroughly incorporated. Immediately remove from the heat to prevent the salmon from overcooking. Spoon into a deep serving bowl and garnish with the salmon strips and the remaining 2 tablespoons dill. Serve immediately.

Serves 4–6

One-Step Potato-Zucchini Pancakes

1 yellow onion, quartered
2 eggs
1 baking potato, about ½ lb (250 g), peeled and cut into chunks
2 small zucchini (courgettes), cut into chunks
½ teaspoon salt
pinch of freshly ground pepper
2 tablespoons all-purpose (plain) flour
vegetable oil, for frying

A colorful alternative to plain potato pancakes. Serve as a side dish to any braised meat or alongside a frittata for brunch. Fresh pear-applesauce makes a nice accompaniment.

In a food processor fitted with the metal blade, combine the onion and eggs and purée until smooth and fluffy. Add the potato and zucchini and, using off-on pulses, process the mixture until finely chopped and still retaining some texture. Add the salt, pepper and flour and briefly process to combine; do not overprocess. Pour the batter into a bowl.

Preheat an oven to 300°F (150°C). Line a baking sheet with a double layer of paper towels. Pour oil to a depth of ½ inch (12 mm) into a large, nonstick frying pan over medium-high heat. Spoon 1 tablespoon of the batter into the pan to test the oil; the batter should hold together and begin to brown. When the oil is hot enough, working in batches, form pancakes by spooning tablespoons of batter into the pan; make sure the pancakes do not touch. Flatten the pancakes with a spatula; they should be about 3 inches (7.5 cm) in diameter. Use the spatula to round and smooth the sides, if necessary. Fry until golden brown on the first side, 3–4 minutes. Flip and fry on the second side until golden brown, 3–4 minutes longer.

Transfer the pancakes to the paper towel–lined baking sheet to drain and place in the oven until all are cooked. Arrange on a warmed platter and serve immediately.

Makes 12–14 pancakes; serves 4–6

Potatoes Lyonnaise

1½ tablespoons unsalted butter

1½ tablespoons olive oil

1 large yellow onion, thinly sliced

2 lb (1 kg) small white or red potatoes, peeled and very thinly sliced

½ cup (4 fl oz/125 ml) chicken stock

salt

freshly ground pepper

2 tablespoons finely chopped fresh parsley

Prepared in the style of Lyons, France, these potatoes are combined with onions that have been sautéed until golden brown and then the dish is finished with chopped parsley. To ensure success, cook the onions to a golden caramel brown first and then add them at the last minute to the sautéed potato slices. Serve with grilled beef, lamb or veal chops.

In a large nonstick frying pan over medium heat, melt ½ tablespoon of the butter with ½ tablespoon of the olive oil. Add the onion slices and sauté, stirring frequently, until golden brown and caramelized, 5–7 minutes. Transfer to a serving bowl.

Add ½ tablespoon each of the remaining butter and olive oil to the same pan over medium-high heat. Add half of the potatoes and cook, turning so they brown on both sides, about 10 minutes. If the potatoes are too dry, add a bit more butter or oil. Transfer to the bowl with the onions. Add the remaining ½ tablespoon each butter and olive oil and brown the remaining potatoes on both sides in the same manner.

Return the onion-potato mixture to the frying pan and add the stock. Raise the heat to high, cover and cook for 2 minutes. Uncover and cook until any remaining stock evaporates. Remove from the heat and season to taste with salt and pepper. Add the parsley and mix to combine. Taste and adjust the seasoning. Transfer to a serving bowl and serve immediately.

Serves 4

Sautéed Potatoes with Apple, Green Onions and Mint

salt to taste, plus 1 teaspoon salt

2 lb (1 kg) white potatoes, peeled

4 tablespoons (2 oz/60 g) unsalted butter

3 tablespoons vegetable oil

6 green (spring) onions, including pale green tops, finely chopped

1 small tart green apple such as pippin or Granny Smith, peeled, cored and cut into 1-inch (2.5-cm) pieces

¼ teaspoon freshly ground pepper

2 tablespoons finely chopped fresh mint, plus whole leaves for garnish

Use a nonstick frying pan and a nonstick spatula for best results. If you do not have a frying pan large enough to accommodate the potatoes in a relatively shallow layer for even browning, use 2 smaller pans. Serve as a side dish to grilled mustard chicken or cheese-laced scrambled eggs. It's also delicious with grilled steak.

*F*ill a large pot three-fourths full with water and bring to a boil over high heat. Add salt to taste and the potatoes and cook for 15 minutes. Drain and cut into 1½-inch (4-cm) pieces. Set aside.

In a large nonstick frying pan over medium heat, melt 2 tablespoons of the butter with 1 tablespoon of the oil. Add the onions and sauté until soft and lightly browned, 3–5 minutes. Transfer the onions to a bowl.

Heat the remaining 2 tablespoons each butter and oil in the same pan over medium heat. Add the potatoes and sauté until golden brown, 6–8 minutes. Using a spatula scrape up the brown bits frequently as the potatoes are cooking. Add the onions and apple to the pan, cover and cook, shaking the pan frequently to prevent burning, for 2 minutes. Remove the cover and stir, scraping the brown bits from the bottom. Continue cooking until the vegetables are very tender, 6–8 minutes longer.

Add the 1 teaspoon salt, the pepper and chopped mint. Taste and adjust the seasoning. Place in a serving bowl, garnish with mint leaves and serve immediately.

Serves 4–6

Sautéed Potatoes with Bell Peppers

1 red bell pepper (capsicum)
1 yellow bell pepper (capsicum)
salt
2 lb (1 kg) red or white potatoes, peeled
    and cut into 1½-inch (4-cm) pieces
2 tablespoons unsalted butter
2 shallots, finely chopped
1 tablespoon olive oil
freshly ground pepper
2 tablespoons finely chopped fresh
    parsley

Here, a colorful potato dish is ribboned with red and yellow peppers, sautéed shallots and fresh herbs.

Roast and peel the bell peppers (see glossary, page 106). Remove the seeds and ribs, then cut the peppers into 1½-inch (4-cm) squares. Set aside.

Fill a large pot three-fourths full with water and bring to a boil over high heat. Add salt to taste and the potatoes and cook until half-cooked, 5–7 minutes. Drain well in a colander and set aside.

In a large nonstick frying pan over medium heat, melt 1 tablespoon of the butter. Add the shallots and sauté until translucent, about 3 minutes. Transfer to a bowl.

Add the remaining 1 tablespoon butter and the olive oil to the same pan and raise the heat to medium-high. Add the potatoes and sauté, turning to brown on all sides, 10–12 minutes. They should be browned and crisp.

Add the red and yellow peppers, shallots, salt and pepper to taste and parsley and toss for 1 minute to combine. Taste and adjust the seasoning. Transfer to a serving bowl and serve immediately.

Serves 4

Grilled Potatoes with Sun-Dried Tomato Pesto

salt

18 small new red potatoes, about 1¾ lb (875 g), unpeeled and well scrubbed

2 tablespoons sun-dried tomato pesto *(recipe on page 10)*

1 tablespoon freshly grated Parmesan cheese

Cooked in aluminum foil, the potatoes steam while the pesto and cheese form a fragrant crust. When you open the foil packages, a delectable aroma fills the air. Serve as a side dish with grilled chicken or fish.

Fill a large pot three-fourths full with water and bring to a boil over high heat. Add salt to taste and the potatoes and cook for 10 minutes. Drain well in a colander and set aside to cool.

Meanwhile, prepare a medium-hot fire in a charcoal grill.

Oil six 6-inch (15-cm) squares of aluminum foil. Arrange 3 potatoes on the center of each foil square. Spoon 1 teaspoon of the pesto atop each portion of potatoes and then sprinkle each portion with ½ teaspoon of the Parmesan cheese. Enclose the potatoes in the foil and seal tightly closed.

Place the foil packages on the grill rack about 3 inches (7.5 cm) from the fire and grill, turning once, until the potatoes are cooked through, 6–8 minutes per side.

Transfer the potato packages to a serving platter. Serve immediately, opening each package carefully with potholder-protected hands just before serving.

Serves 4–6

Potatoes O'Brien

1½ tablespoons unsalted butter

1½ tablespoons olive oil

1 large yellow onion, finely chopped

½ small red bell pepper (capsicum), seeded, deribbed and finely diced

½ small green bell pepper (capsicum), seeded, deribbed and finely diced

2 lb (1 kg) small white or red potatoes, peeled and cut into ½-inch (12-mm) pieces

salt

freshly ground pepper

2 tablespoons finely chopped fresh parsley

Jack's, a restaurant in New York famous in the early 1900s for after-theater dining, originated these potatoes. There are now so many versions of this dish that it is nearly impossible to get the same recipe from more than one person. This version makes a zesty side dish to eggs, roast chicken or beef. You can vary the recipe by adding yellow and orange peppers or by including a chili pepper if you prefer spicy flavors.

In a large frying pan over medium-high heat, melt ½ tablespoon of the butter with ½ tablespoon of the olive oil. Add the onion and sauté, stirring frequently, until golden brown and just beginning to caramelize, 5–7 minutes. Add the red and green bell pepper and sauté for 3–5 minutes longer. Transfer to a serving bowl.

Add ½ tablespoon each of the remaining butter and olive oil to the same frying pan. Add half of the potatoes and cook, turning to brown on all sides, 5–7 minutes. If the potatoes are too dry, add a bit more butter or oil. Transfer to the bowl with the onion mixture. Add the remaining ½ tablespoon each butter and olive oil and brown the remaining potatoes on all sides in the same manner.

Return the mixture to the pan. Raise the heat so the mixture quickly warms throughout. Remove from the heat and season to taste with salt and pepper. Add the parsley and mix to combine. Taste and adjust the seasoning. Transfer to a serving bowl and serve immediately.

Serves 4–6

Straw Potato Leek Cake

2 lb (1 kg) white potatoes, peeled
3 tablespoons unsalted butter
3 tablespoons olive oil
2 leeks, including pale green tops, trimmed, carefully washed and finely chopped
1 teaspoon salt
½ teaspoon freshly ground pepper

If you like, turn the cooked pancake out onto a flameproof platter, sprinkle with crisp bacon pieces and a few tablespoons grated Gruyère cheese and slip under a preheated broiler (griller) for a minute or so to melt the cheese. A sprinkling of your favorite herbs— parsley, basil, chives—makes a pretty garnish.

*Place the potatoes in a bowl, add water to cover and let stand for 5 minutes to remove excess starch, changing the water once when it becomes cloudy. Drain in a colander.

In a food processor fitted with the shredding disk, shred the potatoes. Alternatively, use a mandoline or a hand-held grater/ shredder. The thicker you shred them, the crunchier the cake will be. Place in a kitchen towel and wring tightly to remove all moisture. Transfer to a bowl.

In a frying pan over medium heat, melt 1 tablespoon of the butter with 1 tablespoon of the olive oil. Add the leeks and sauté until softened, about 5 minutes. Season with the salt and pepper. Add the leeks to the potatoes and stir well.

In a large nonstick frying pan over medium-high heat, warm the remaining 2 tablespoons each butter and oil. Add the potato mixture and flatten firmly with a spatula. Cover and cook over medium-high heat until browned on the underside, 3–5 minutes. Invert a plate over the pan and, holding the plate firmly in place, invert the pan. Slide the pancake back into the pan, browned side up. Flatten firmly again, cover and cook until browned and crisp on the second side, 3–5 minutes longer. Invert a warmed round serving platter on the pan and invert as directed above. Cut into wedges and serve hot.

Serves 4–6

Sautéed Potatoes, Mushrooms and Goat Cheese

salt

2 lb (1 kg) red or white potatoes, peeled and cut into 1-inch (2.5-cm) pieces

3 tablespoons unsalted butter

2 tablespoons olive oil

1 lb (500 g) small fresh mushrooms, quartered

2 cloves garlic, minced

freshly ground pepper

½ cup (2 oz/60 g) crumbled fresh goat cheese

1 tablespoon finely chopped fresh basil

1 tablespoon finely chopped fresh chives

Bits of creamy fresh goat cheese are added to this savory side dish just before it is brought to the table. Prepare it just before serving, so the potatoes are at their crispest. These are a big hit served with any simple grilled main course such as steaks, salmon fillets or lamb chops.

*F*ill a large pot three-fourths full with water and bring to a boil over high heat. Add salt to taste and the potatoes and cook for 5 minutes. Drain well in a colander and set aside.

In a large nonstick frying pan over medium-high heat, melt 1 tablespoon of the butter with 1 tablespoon of the olive oil. Add the mushrooms and sauté until lightly browned, about 5 minutes. Add the garlic and cook for 30 seconds. Transfer to a bowl and cover to keep warm.

Add the remaining 2 tablespoons butter and 1 tablespoon olive oil to the same pan over medium-high heat. Add the potatoes and sauté, turning to brown all sides, 10–15 minutes. If they are too dry, add a bit more butter or oil.

When the potatoes are browned, add the mushrooms, being careful to leave behind any excess liquid that has drained to the bottom of the bowl. Mix briefly and transfer to a serving bowl. Season to taste with salt and pepper and then toss in the goat cheese, basil and chives. Serve immediately.

Serves 4–6

Roasted Garlic Mashed Potatoes

2 lb (1 kg) white, red, yellow-fleshed or baking potatoes, peeled and cut into 3-inch (7.5-cm) pieces

salt

1 tablespoon roasted garlic purée (recipe on page 10), or to taste

2 tablespoons unsalted butter, cut into small pieces

2 tablespoons olive oil

⅔ cup (5 fl oz/160 ml) half-and-half, heated

white pepper

2 tablespoons chopped fresh parsley, optional

These mashed potatoes are a real crowd pleaser. They can be made up to 1 hour in advance and kept warm in the top pan of a double boiler or in a heatproof bowl placed over a pan of simmering water. Serve with grilled salmon, roast chicken or turkey, or a hearty stew.

To remove excess starch, place the potatoes in a large bowl and add water to cover; let stand for 5 minutes, then drain.

Fill a large pot three-fourths full with water and bring to a boil over high heat. Add salt to taste and the potatoes and cook until tender when pierced with a fork, about 15 minutes. Drain well in a colander and return the potatoes to the pot over high heat to dry, turning to prevent scorching, until all the moisture evaporates, 1–2 minutes.

If you are serving the mashed potatoes immediately, place a ricer or a food mill over a large bowl. If you are holding the mashed potatoes for a while before serving, place the ricer or mill over the top pan of a 2-qt (2-l) double boiler. Alternatively, use a heatproof bowl placed over a pan of hot water (but not touching the water). Put the potato chunks and garlic purée through the ricer or mill. Add the butter and olive oil to the bowl, then slowly add the half-and-half, stirring constantly with a large spoon until the potatoes are very creamy but not soupy. Add salt and white pepper to taste.

Transfer to a serving bowl and garnish with the parsley if desired. Serve immediately.

Serves 4

White Potato Purée

salt

1 lb (500 g) parsnips, peeled and cut
into 2-inch (5-cm) pieces

1 small yellow onion, quartered

1 clove garlic

1 lb (500 g) white potatoes, peeled and
cut into 2-inch (5-cm) pieces

1 lb (500 g) turnips, peeled and cut into
2-inch (5-cm) pieces

5 tablespoons (2½ oz/80 g) unsalted
butter, at room temperature, cut into
small pieces

¾ cup (6 fl oz/180 ml) half-and-half or
heavy (double) cream, heated

white pepper

2 tablespoons chopped fresh parsley

Turnips and parsnips give this wintry dish extra flavor. For a more family-style presentation, place the purée in a baking dish, sprinkle with Parmesan cheese and bake in a preheated 350°F (180°C) oven for 20 minutes.

*F*ill a large pot three-fourths full with water and bring to a boil over high heat. Add salt to taste, the parsnips, onion and garlic and cook for 5 minutes. Add the potatoes and turnips and cook until tender when pierced with a fork, about 15 minutes longer. (If some vegetables are done before others, transfer them to a bowl.)

Drain all the vegetables in a colander; discard the onion and garlic. Return the vegetables to the pot over high heat to dry, turning to prevent scorching, until all the moisture evaporates, 1–2 minutes.

If you are serving the purée immediately, place a ricer or food mill over a large bowl. If you are holding the purée for a while before serving, place the ricer or food mill over the top pan of a 2-qt (2-l) double boiler, or a heatproof bowl placed over a pan of hot water (but not touching the water). Put the vegetable cubes through the ricer or mill, discarding any tough pieces that won't go through. Add the butter to the bowl and slowly pour in the half-and-half, stirring constantly with a large spoon until the mixture is very creamy but not soupy. Season to taste with salt and white pepper.

Transfer to a serving bowl and garnish with the parsley. Serve immediately.

Serves 6–8

Herbed New Potatoes with White Wine Glaze

1½ lb (750 g) small new potatoes,
   unpeeled and well scrubbed
2 tablespoons unsalted butter
2 tablespoons dry white wine
2 teaspoons finely chopped fresh chives
1 tablespoon finely chopped fresh mint
¼ teaspoon salt
⅛ teaspoon white pepper

Peeling the potatoes around the center creates an attractive presentation ideal for a special meal. The herbed white wine glaze adds lively flavor.

*U*sing a sharp knife, peel a ring of skin from around the center of each potato. Pour water to a depth of 1 inch (2.5 cm) into a steamer pan. Put the steamer rack in place and bring the water to a boil. Using tongs place the potatoes on the rack, cover and steam over medium heat until tender, 15–20 minutes.

Just before the potatoes are ready, in a small saucepan over medium heat, melt the butter. Add the wine, chives, mint, salt and white pepper. Stir to mix, then taste and adjust the seasoning.

Transfer the potatoes to a serving bowl and pour the butter mixture over the top. Mix gently to coat the potatoes evenly and serve immediately.

Serves 4

Mashed Potatoes with Horseradish and Leeks

2 lb (1 kg) white, red, yellow-fleshed or baking potatoes, peeled and cut into 3-inch (7.5-cm) pieces

2 tablespoons unsalted butter, plus 3 tablespoons unsalted butter, cut into small pieces

1 leek (white and light green tops), trimmed, carefully washed and finely chopped

salt

2 teaspoons prepared horseradish

¾ cup (6 fl oz/180 ml) half-and-half, heated

white pepper

Prepared horseradish, sold in jars in the vegetable section of many markets, works better than fresh horseradish root for this dish. Serve these zesty potatoes alongside grilled salmon fillets or roast pork loin. Chopped dark green leek tops make an attractive garnish.

*T*o remove excess starch, place the potatoes in a large bowl and add water to cover; let stand for 5 minutes, then drain.

Meanwhile, in a nonstick frying pan over medium heat, melt the 2 tablespoons butter. Add the leek and sauté, stirring often, until soft, 5–7 minutes. Set aside.

Fill a large pot three-fourths full with water and bring to a boil. Add salt to taste and the potatoes and boil until tender when pierced with a fork, about 15 minutes. Drain well in a colander and return to the pot over high heat to dry, turning to prevent scorching, until all the moisture evaporates, 1–2 minutes.

If you are serving the potatoes immediately, place a ricer or a food mill over a large bowl. If you are holding the potatoes for up to 1 hour before serving, place the ricer or mill over the top pan of a 2-qt (2-l) double boiler, or a heatproof bowl placed over a pan of hot water (but not touching the water). Put the potatoes through the ricer or mill. Add the butter pieces and horseradish to the bowl and slowly add the half-and-half, stirring constantly until the potatoes are creamy but not soupy. Mix in the leek and salt and white pepper to taste. Transfer to a serving bowl and serve immediately.

Serves 4

Gingered Yam and Squash Purée

2 yam-type sweet potatoes, about ½ lb (250 g) each

2 teaspoons vegetable oil

1 butternut squash, about 2 lb (1 kg), peeled, seeded and cut into slices 1 inch (2.5 cm) thick

1½ teaspoons finely chopped fresh ginger

1 tablespoon maple syrup

2 tablespoons unsalted butter

salt

white pepper

2 tablespoons finely chopped fresh parsley

Fresh ginger and maple syrup add an unexpected surprise to this golden orange purée. This is pretty on a holiday buffet and is excellent served alongside ham or turkey.

*P*reheat an oven to 400°F (200°C).

Scrub the sweet potatoes to remove all dirt, then dry thoroughly with a kitchen towel. Rub each sweet potato with 1 teaspoon of the oil to coat evenly. Place on an ungreased baking sheet in the middle of the oven. Bake for 30 minutes. Prick the skin in several places with fork tines and continue to bake until tender when pierced with a knife or skewer, about 30 minutes longer. Remove from the oven and let cool.

While the sweet potatoes are baking, pour water to a depth of 1 inch (2.5 cm) in the bottom of a large steamer. Put the steamer rack in place and bring the water to a boil. Using tongs place the squash slices on the rack, cover and steam over medium heat until tender when pierced with a fork, 15–20 minutes. Remove from the heat and set aside.

When the sweet potatoes are cool enough to handle, cut in half, scoop out the pulp from the skins, and place in a food processor fitted with the metal blade. Add the squash, ginger, maple syrup and butter and process until puréed. Add salt and white pepper to taste.

Spoon into a serving bowl, garnish with the parsley and serve immediately.

Serves 4–6

Creamy Red Potato Salad with Celery Seeds

salt

3 lb (1.5 kg) red potatoes, unpeeled and well scrubbed

FOR THE DRESSING:

¾ cup (6 fl oz/180 ml) sour cream

¾ cup (6 fl oz/180 ml) mayonnaise

2 celery stalks, finely diced

1 tablespoon celery seeds

2 tablespoons chopped green (spring) onion, plus 1 tablespoon finely chopped green onion

5 tablespoons chopped fresh parsley

1 teaspoon dry mustard

½ teaspoon salt

¼ teaspoon white pepper

The red skins on the potatoes add extra color and texture to this salad. Fresh celery and celery seeds add a double dose of flavor. Serve on a bed of mixed greens, if you like. This salad is perfect with cold roast beef or cold chicken.

*F*ill a large pot three-fourths full with water and bring to a boil over high heat. Add salt to taste and the potatoes and cook until tender but slightly resistant when pierced with a fork, 25–30 minutes. Drain and let cool, then cut the unpeeled potatoes into 1-inch (2.5-cm) cubes. Place in a bowl.

To make the dressing, in a small bowl combine the sour cream, mayonnaise, celery, celery seeds, the 2 tablespoons green onion, 4 tablespoons of the parsley, mustard, salt and white pepper. Using a large spoon mix well.

Pour the dressing over the potatoes and mix gently until evenly coated. Taste and adjust the seasoning. Transfer to a serving bowl and garnish with the remaining 1 tablespoon parsley and the 1 tablespoon finely chopped green onion.

Before serving, cover and refrigerate for 1–2 hours to chill and blend the flavors.

Serves 6–8

Warm Potato and Shrimp Salad

salt

2½ lb (1.25 kg) red or yellow-fleshed
  potatoes, unpeeled and well scrubbed

1 lb (500 g) cooked, peeled and
  deveined shrimp (prawns), cut into
  1-inch (2.5-cm) pieces

FOR THE DRESSING:

1 shallot, finely chopped

1 clove garlic, minced

1 tablespoon chopped fresh parsley

1 tablespoon chopped fresh chives

1 teaspoon plus 2 tablespoons chopped
  fresh dill

1 teaspoon Dijon mustard

2 tablespoons fresh lemon juice

2 tablespoons white wine vinegar

¾ cup (6 fl oz/180 ml) olive oil

½ teaspoon salt

¼ teaspoon freshly ground pepper

Sweet pink shrimp and creamy yellow potatoes team up in this sophisticated main-course salad. An assertive lemon-herb dressing brings out the natural flavors of the principal ingredients. If you are starting with uncooked shrimp, you will need about 1¼ lb (625 g). Boil them until they turn pink and begin to curl, about 3 minutes. Then drain, immerse in cold water to cool, drain again, and peel and devein. If you like, serve the salad mounded on lettuce and garnished with lemon wedges.

Fill a large pot three-fourths full with water and bring to a boil over high heat. Add salt to taste and the potatoes and cook until tender but slightly resistant when pierced with a fork, 25–30 minutes. Drain and let cool slightly.

Holding the potatoes under cold water, peel them. Cut into ½-inch (12-mm) cubes and place in a bowl. Add the shrimp.

To make the dressing, in a small bowl combine the shallot, garlic, parsley, chives, the 1 teaspoon dill, mustard, lemon juice and vinegar. Whisk until well mixed. Slowly pour in the olive oil, whisking continuously until blended. Add the salt and pepper. Taste and adjust the seasoning.

Pour the dressing over the potatoes and shrimp and mix gently until evenly coated. Taste and adjust the seasoning.

Transfer to a serving bowl and garnish with the 2 tablespoons dill. Serve immediately.

Serves 6

Potato Salad Tonnato

A creamy tuna dressing, adapted from a classic Italian sauce for veal, accents chunks of red potato and crisp green beans. This is a substantial potato salad that can be served on a summer buffet with cold poached salmon and a cherry tomato salad.

salt

3 lb (1.5 kg) red potatoes, unpeeled and well scrubbed

1 lb (500 g) green beans, trimmed and cut into 1-inch (2.5-cm) lengths

FOR THE DRESSING:

1 cup (8 fl oz/250 ml) mayonnaise

¼ cup (2 fl oz/60 ml) sour cream

1 can (6½ oz/200 g) white-meat tuna packed in water, drained

3 tablespoons fresh lemon juice

2 teaspoons anchovy paste

¼ teaspoon white pepper

FOR GARNISH:

2 tablespoons capers, rinsed and well drained

yellow pear or red cherry tomato halves

Niçoise olives

*F*ill a large pot three-fourths full with water and bring to a boil over high heat. Add salt to taste and the potatoes and cook until tender but slightly resistant when pierced with a fork, 25–30 minutes. Drain well and let cool, then cut into 1½-inch (4-cm) cubes and place in a bowl.

Meanwhile, fill a saucepan three-fourths full with water and bring to a boil over high heat. Add the green beans and cook until tender but slightly resistant when pierced with a fork, 5–7 minutes. Drain and immerse in cold water to stop the cooking. Drain well again and add to the bowl holding the potatoes.

In a food processor fitted with the metal blade or in a blender, combine all the ingredients for the dressing. Process until creamy.

Pour the dressing over the potatoes and mix gently until evenly coated. Taste and adjust the seasoning. Transfer to a deep serving bowl and garnish with the capers, tomato halves and olives. Refrigerate for 1–2 hours before serving to chill and blend the flavors.

Serves 6–8

97

Warm Potato, Sausage and Goat Cheese Salad

1½ lb (750 g) fresh sausages of your
choice, such as sweet or hot Italian or
bockwurst
salt
2 lb (1 kg) white, red or yellow-fleshed
potatoes, unpeeled and well scrubbed

FOR THE DRESSING:
1 shallot, finely chopped
1 clove garlic, minced
1 tablespoon chopped fresh parsley
1 tablespoon chopped fresh chives
1 teaspoon chopped fresh basil
1 teaspoon Dijon mustard
1 tablespoon fresh lemon juice
3 tablespoons white wine vinegar
¾ cup (6 fl oz/180 ml) olive oil
½ teaspoon salt
¼ teaspoon freshly ground pepper

¾ cup (3 oz/90 g) crumbled fresh
goat cheese
4 tablespoons chopped fresh parsley
red-leaf lettuce leaves

Here is a hearty main-course salad that is ideal served alongside a bowl of hot soup on a chilly day. Add the goat cheese just before serving, so the chunks do not melt into the dressing.

Preheat a broiler (griller), or prepare a fire in a charcoal grill. Place the sausages on a broiler pan or grill rack and broil or grill, turning to cook evenly, until done, about 10 minutes, depending upon the sausage. Let cool, then cut on the diagonal into slices 1 inch (2.5 cm) thick. Place in a bowl.

Meanwhile, fill a large pot three-fourths full with water and bring to a boil. Add salt to taste and the potatoes and boil until tender but slightly resistant when pierced, 25–30 minutes. Drain and let cool slightly. Holding the potatoes under cold water, peel them. Cut into 1-inch (2.5-cm) cubes and add to the sausages.

To make the dressing, in a small bowl combine the shallot, garlic, parsley, chives, basil, mustard, lemon juice and vinegar. Whisk to mix well. Slowly add the olive oil, whisking continuously. Add the salt and pepper. Taste for seasoning.

Pour the dressing over the potatoes and sausage and mix gently. Taste again for seasoning. Add the cheese and 2 tablespoons of the parsley and toss gently.

Line a serving dish with lettuce leaves and spoon the salad on top. Garnish with the remaining 2 tablespoons parsley and serve immediately.

Serves 6

German Potato Salad

salt to taste, plus ½ teaspoon salt

2 lb (1 kg) red or white potatoes, unpeeled and well scrubbed

6 bacon slices, cut into 1-inch (2.5-cm) pieces

6 tablespoons (3 fl oz/90 ml) olive oil

1 yellow onion, thinly sliced

2 teaspoons all-purpose (plain) flour

1 tablespoon sugar

¼ teaspoon freshly ground pepper

½ cup (4 fl oz/125 ml) water

¼ cup (2 fl oz/60 ml) cider vinegar

6 tablespoons finely chopped fresh parsley

Serve this warm, directly from the pan, for a comforting winter-time lunch. Olive oil replaces the traditional bacon drippings in the dressing for a lighter dish. A glass of red wine makes a fine accompaniment.

*F*ill a large pot three-fourths full with water and bring to a boil over high heat. Add salt to taste and the potatoes and cook until tender but slightly resistant when pierced with a fork, 25–30 minutes. Drain and let cool slightly, then peel and cut into slices 1 inch (2.5 cm) thick. Place in a serving bowl.

In a frying pan over medium heat, sauté the bacon until crisp. Using a slotted spoon remove the bacon and set aside. Discard the drippings.

In the same pan warm the olive oil over medium heat. Add the onion and sauté until soft and lightly browned, about 5 minutes. Stir in the flour, sugar, the ½ teaspoon salt, pepper and water and continue cooking until the dressing begins to thicken, 3–5 minutes. Add the vinegar, the reserved bacon and 4 tablespoons of the parsley and cook for 1 minute longer. Taste and adjust the seasoning.

Pour the dressing over the potatoes and mix gently to coat evenly. Garnish with the remaining 2 tablespoons parsley and serve immediately.

Serves 4–6

Potato Salad with Sun-Dried Tomato Cream

salt

2½ lb (1.25 kg) white potatoes, unpeeled and well scrubbed

FOR THE DRESSING:

½ cup (4 fl oz/125 ml) sour cream

½ cup (4 oz/125 g) nonfat plain yogurt

2 tablespoons sun-dried tomato pesto (*recipe on page 10*)

1 tablespoon white wine vinegar

1 teaspoon balsamic vinegar

1 teaspoon Dijon mustard

2 tablespoons capers, rinsed and well drained

¼ teaspoon salt

pinch of freshly ground pepper

2 tablespoons chopped fresh parsley, plus extra for garnish

This is a wonderful side dish to accompany cold meats, cheeses and assorted fresh vegetables such as carrots, asparagus or green beans.

*F*ill a large pot three-fourths full with water and bring to a boil over high heat. Add salt to taste and the potatoes and cook until tender but slightly resistant when pierced with a fork, 25–30 minutes. Drain and let cool slightly, then peel and cut into slices or cubes 1½ inches (4 cm) thick. Place in a bowl.

In a small bowl combine all the ingredients for the dressing and mix well. Taste and adjust the seasoning.

Pour the dressing over the potatoes and mix gently until evenly coated. Taste again for seasoning. Transfer to a serving bowl and garnish with chopped parsley. Refrigerate for 1–2 hours before serving to chill and blend the flavors.

Serves 6

Glossary

The following glossary defines terms specifically as they relate to potato cookery, including major and unusual ingredients and basic techniques.

ANCHOVY PASTE
Smooth paste made from preserved fillets of the tiny saltwater fish, combined with oil and packed in squeeze tubes and jars.

BELL PEPPERS
See Peppers.

BREAD CRUMBS, DRIED
Dried bread crumbs have many uses, including forming a crunchy golden topping on potato gratins. To make dried bread crumbs, choose a good-quality, rustic-style loaf made of unbleached wheat flour, with a firm, coarse-textured crumb. Cut away the crusts and crumble the bread by hand or in a blender or a food processor fitted with the metal blade. Spread the crumbs on a baking sheet and dry slowly, about 1 hour, in an oven set at its lowest temperature. Store in a covered container at room temperature. Dried bread crumbs, usually fine-textured, are also sold prepackaged in food markets.

BUTTER, UNSALTED
For the recipes in this book, unsalted butter is preferred. It allows the cook greater leeway in seasoning recipes to taste.

Clarifying Butter
Butter is often clarified—that is, its milk solids and water are removed—when it is to be used for cooking at high temperatures or as a sauce. To clarify butter, melt it in a small, heavy saucepan over very low heat; watch carefully to avoid burning. Remove

from the heat and let sit briefly. Then, using a spoon, skim off and discard the foam from the surface. Finally, carefully pour off the clear yellow oil, leaving the milky solids and water behind in the pan. Clarified butter can be refrigerated for up to 1 month or frozen for 2 months.

CAPERS
Small, pickled buds of a bush common to the Mediterranean, used whole as a savory flavoring or garnish.

CAVIARS AND ROES
All manner of fish eggs, or roes, are preserved with salt, which highlights their subtle, briny flavor. The term *caviar* is traditionally reserved for sturgeon roe, which is the finest of the fish roes. Other commonly available roes are carp roe and salmon roe. Eaten as special-occasion hors d'oeuvres in their own right, caviars and roes can also be used along with sour cream or crème fraîche as garnishes for baked potatoes. A good selection may be found in some specialty-food stores and delicatessens.

CAYENNE
Very hot ground spice derived from dried cayenne chili peppers.

CELERY SEEDS
Small, dried pale green seeds of the familiar vegetable, sold in the spice section of food markets and used whole as a seasoning to add a subtle celery flavor.

CHILI PEPPERS
See Peppers.

CREAM, HEAVY
Whipping cream with a butterfat content of at least 36 percent. For the best flavor and cooking properties, purchase 100 percent natural fresh cream with a short shelf life printed on the carton,

CHEESES
In its many forms, cheese makes an excellent ingredient in or garnish for potato dishes. For the best selection and finest quality, buy cheese from a well-stocked food store or delicatessen that offers a wide variety and has a frequent turnover of product.

Cheddar
Firm, smooth-textured whole milk cheese, pale yellow-white to deep yellow-orange and ranging in taste from mild and sweet when fresh to rich and sharply tangy when aged.

Dolcelatte
Literally "sweet milk." Italian mild, creamy, blue-veined variety of Gorgonzola.

Feta
White, salty, sharp-tasting cheese made from sheep's or goat's milk, with a crumbly, creamy-to-dry consistency.

Fontina
Firm, creamy, delicate Italian cheese (below) with a slightly nutty taste; made from cow's milk. The best is from the Aosta Valley of northwestern Italy.

Goat Cheese
Most cheeses made from goat's milk are fresh and creamy, with a distinctive sharp tang; they are sold shaped into small rounds or logs. Some are coated with pepper, ash or mixtures of

herbs, which mildly flavors them. Also known by the French term *chèvre*.

Gorgonzola
Italian variety of creamy, blue-veined cheese (below). Other creamy blue cheeses may be substituted.

Gruyère
Variety of Swiss cheese with a firm, smooth texture, small holes and a relatively strong flavor.

Monterey Jack
Semisoft white melting cheese with a mild flavor and buttery texture.

Parmesan
Hard, thick-crusted Italian cow's milk cheese with a sharp, salty, full flavor resulting from at least two years of aging. The finest Italian variety is designated parmigiano-reggiano. Buy in block form, to grate fresh as needed, rather than already grated.

avoiding long-lasting varieties that have been processed by ultra-pasteurization methods. In Britain, use double cream.

CREAM OF TARTAR
Acidic powder extracted during wine making that is used as an additive to egg whites, serving both to stabilize the egg whites and to increase their heat tolerance.

CRÈME FRAÎCHE
French-style lightly soured and thickened fresh cream, generally used as a topping or garnish for savory or sweet dishes. Increasingly available in food markets, although a similar product may be prepared at home by stirring 2 teaspoons well-drained sour cream into 1 cup (8 fl oz/250 ml) lightly whipped heavy (double) cream. Or, to make your own crème fraîche, stir 1 teaspoon cultured buttermilk into 1 cup (8 fl oz/250 ml) heavy (double) cream. Cover tightly and leave at warm room temperature until thickened, about 12 hours. Refrigerate until ready to serve. Will keep for up to 1 week.

EGGS, SEPARATING
To separate an egg, crack the shell in half by tapping it against the side of a bowl and then breaking it apart with your fingers. Holding the shell halves over the bowl, gently transfer the whole yolk back and forth between them, letting the clear white drop away into the bowl. Take care not to cut into the yolk with the edges of the shell (the whites will not beat properly if they contain any yolk). Transfer the yolk to another bowl.

HALF-AND-HALF
A commercial dairy product consisting of half milk and half light cream. In Britain known as half cream.

HERBS
Many fresh and dried herbs alike can be used to embellish the relatively mild, earthy flavor of potatoes, including:

Basil
Sweet, spicy herb popular in Italian and French cooking.

Chives
Long, thin green shoot with a mild flavor reminiscent of the onion, to which it is related. Although chives are available dried in the herb-and-spice section of food stores, fresh chives possess the best flavor.

Cilantro
Green, leafy herb resembling flat-leaf (Italian) parsley, with a sharp, aromatic, somewhat astringent flavor. Popular in Latin American and Asian cuisines. Also called fresh coriander and commonly referred to as Chinese parsley.

Dill
Fine, feathery leaves with a sweet, aromatic flavor. Sold fresh or dried.

Mint
Refreshing herb available in many varieties, with spearmint the most common. Used fresh to flavor a broad range of savory and sweet ingredients.

Parsley
This popular fresh herb is available in two varieties, the readily available curly-leaf type and a flat-leaf type (below). The latter, also known as Italian parsley, has a more pronounced flavor and is preferred.

Thyme
Fragrant, clean-tasting, small-leaved herb popular fresh or dried as a seasoning for poultry, light meats, seafood or vegetables. A variety called lemon thyme imparts a pleasant lemon scent to foods.

Chopping Fresh Herbs
Wash the herbs under cold running water and thoroughly shake dry. If the herb has leaves attached along woody stems, pull the leaves from the stems; otherwise, as in the case of the parsley shown here, hold the stems together. Gather up the leaves into a tight, compact bunch. Using a chef's knife, carefully cut across the bunch to chop the leaves coarsely. Discard the stems.

For more finely chopped herbs, gather the coarsely chopped leaves together. Steadying the top of the knife blade with one hand, chop the herbs, rocking the blade and moving it back and forth in an arc until the desired fineness is reached.

Crushing Dried Herbs
If using dried herbs, it is best to crush them first in the palm of the hand to release their flavor. Or warm them in a frying pan and crush using a mortar and pestle.

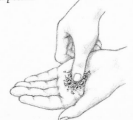

LEEKS

Moderately flavored member of the onion family, long and cylindrical in shape with a pale white root end and dark green leaves. Select small to medium, firm, unblemished leeks. Grown in sandy soil, the leafy-topped, multilayered vegetables require thorough cleaning.

Trim off the tough ends of the dark green leaves and, starting about 1 inch (2.5 cm) from the root end, slit the leek lengthwise. Then vigorously swish the leek in a basin or sink of cold water. Drain and rinse again, making sure that no dirt remains between the leaves.

MUSTARDS

Mustard is available in three forms: whole seeds, powdered (referred to as dry mustard) and prepared, which is made from powdered or coarsely ground mustard seed mixed with liquid such as vinegar or wine. Spicy Dijon mustard is made in Dijon, France, from powdered dark brown mustard seeds (unless otherwise marked *blanc*) and white wine or wine vinegar. Pale in color, fairly hot and sharp tasting, true Dijon mustard and non-French blends labeled "Dijon-style" are available in most food markets and specialty-food stores.

OILS

Oils provide a medium in which potatoes may be sautéed or deep-fried without sticking. Vegetable oils derived from corn or safflower seeds are used when high frying temperatures are necessary because they can tolerate extreme heat without burning and they lack flavor. Olive oil, on the other hand, is prized for its fruity taste and golden to pale green hue. Many brands of olive oil, varying in color and strength of flavor, are now available; choose one that suits your taste. Olive oil nonstick cooking spray provides a subtle hint of the oil's flavor with few of its calories. Store all oils in airtight containers away from heat and light.

OLIVES, NIÇOISE

Good-quality small, brine-cured, brown to black olives from Provence. Available in French-type delicatessens, specialty-food shops and well-stocked markets.

PAPRIKA

Powdered spice derived from the dried paprika pepper; popular in several European cuisines and available in sweet, mild and hot forms. Hungarian paprika is the best, but Spanish paprika, which is mild, may also be used. Buy in small quantities from shops with a high turnover, to ensure a fresh, flavorful supply.

PARSNIPS

Root vegetable similar in shape and texture to the carrot, but with ivory flesh and an appealingly sweet flavor.

PEPPERCORNS

Pepper, the most common of all savory spices, is best purchased as whole peppercorns, to be ground

PEPPERS

The widely varied pepper family ranges in form and taste from large, mild bell peppers (capsicums) to tiny, spicy-hot chilies.

Fresh, sweet-fleshed bell peppers (below) are most common in the unripe green form, although ripened red or yellow varieties are also available. Creamy pale yellow, orange and purple-black types may also be found.

Bell Pepper

Red, ripe chilies are sold fresh and dried. Fresh green chilies include the mild-to-hot, dark green poblano, which resembles a tapered, triangular bell pepper; the long, mild Anaheim, or New Mexican; and the small, fiery serrano and jalapeño. When handling chilies, wear kitchen gloves to prevent any cuts or abrasions on your hands from contacting the peppers' volatile oils; wash your hands well with warm, soapy water, and take special care not to touch your eyes or other sensitive areas.

Serrano Chilies

Poblano Chili

Seeding Raw Peppers

To prepare a raw bell pepper— shown here—or chili pepper, cut it in half lengthwise with a sharp knife. Pull out the stem section from each half, along with the cluster of seeds attached to it. Remove any remaining seeds, along with any thin white membranes, or ribs, to which they are attached.

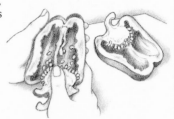

Roasting Peppers

When a recipe calls for roasted chilies or bell peppers, place the whole peppers in a shallow pan and place under a preheated broiler (griller) 6 inches (15 cm) from the heat; or place directly on a grill rack the same distance from the fire. Using tongs to turn the peppers, roast until evenly blackened.

Transfer the peppers to a brown paper bag, close tightly and leave for 10 minutes. Remove from the bag and, using your fingertips, peel off the blackened skins; then slit open and remove the stems, seeds and ribs.

in a pepper mill as needed, or coarsely crushed using a mortar and pestle or the side of a heavy knife. Pungent black peppercorns derive from slightly underripe pepper berries, whose hulls oxidize as they dry. Milder white peppercorns come from fully ripened berries, with the black husks removed before drying.

PUMPKIN PIE SPICE
Commercial blend of cinnamon, cloves, ginger and nutmeg, commonly used to flavor pumpkin pies and also to season some sweet potato dishes.

RED PEPPER FLAKES
Coarse flakes of dried red chilies, including seeds, which add moderately hot flavor to the foods they season.

SALMON, SMOKED
Purchase freshly sliced smoked salmon from a good-quality delicatessen or fish market. Lox, which is a salt-cured salmon, and Nova, which is a cold-smoked salmon, are commonly sold in Jewish delicatessens; they have oilier textures and in most cases are not acceptable substitutes for smoked salmon.

SHALLOT
Small member of the onion family with brown skin, white flesh tinged with purple, and a flavor resembling a cross between sweet onion and garlic.

STOCK
Flavorful liquid derived from slowly simmering chicken, meat, fish or vegetables in water, along with herbs and aromatic vegetables. Used as the primary cooking liquid or moistening and flavoring agent in many recipes. Stock may be made fairly easily at home, to be frozen for future use.

SHRIMP
Raw shrimp (prawns) are generally sold with the heads already removed but the shells still intact. Before cooking, they are usually peeled and their thin, veinlike intestinal tracts removed.

Using your thumbs, split open the shrimp's thin shell along the concave side, between its two rows of legs. Peel away the shell, taking care to leave the last segment with tail fin intact and attached to the meat.

Using a small, sharp knife, carefully make a shallow slit along the peeled shrimp's back, just deep enough to expose the long, usually dark, veinlike intestinal tract. With the tip of the knife or your fingers, lift up and pull out the vein, discarding it.

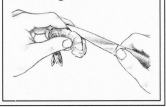

Many good-quality canned stocks or broths, in regular or concentrated form, are also available; they tend to be saltier than homemade stock, however, so recipes in which they are used should be carefully tasted for seasoning. Excellent stocks may also be found in the freezer section of quality food stores.

SUN-DRIED TOMATOES
When sliced crosswise or halved, then dried in the sun, tomatoes develop an intense, sweet-tart flavor and a pleasantly chewy texture that enhance savory recipes. Available either dry or packed in oil with or without herbs and spices. Sold in specialty-food shops and well-stocked food stores.

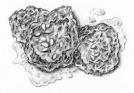

TOMATILLO SALSA
Mexican sauce made from the small, green vegetable-fruit resembling, but not actually related to, the tomato, in combination with chilies, herbs and other seasonings. Can be found fresh in the refrigerated case or bottled in the Mexican-foods section of ethnic food shops or well-stocked markets.

TOMATOES
During summer, when tomatoes are in season, use the best sun-ripened tomatoes you can find. At other times of year, plum tomatoes, sometimes called Roma or egg tomatoes, are likely to have the best flavor and texture. To peel fresh tomatoes, bring a saucepan filled with water to a boil. Using a small, sharp knife, cut out the core from the stem end of the tomato. Then cut a shallow X in the skin at the tomato's base. Submerge for about 20 seconds in boiling water, then remove and dip in a bowl of cold water. Starting at the X, peel the skin from the tomato. To seed a tomato, cut it in half crosswise. Squeeze gently to force out the seed sacks.

TURNIPS
Small, creamy white root vegetable, tinged purple or green at its crown, with firm, pungent yet slightly sweet flesh. Choose smaller turnips that feel heavy for their size and are firm to the touch.

VINEGAR
Literally "sour" wine, vinegar results when certain strains of yeast cause wine—or some other alcoholic liquid such as apple cider—to ferment for a second time, turning it acidic. The best-quality wine vinegars begin with good-quality wine. Red wine vinegar, like the wine from which it is made, has a more robust flavor than vinegar produced from white wine. Balsamic vinegar, a specialty of Modena, Italy, is a vinegar made from reduced grape juice and aged for many years.

WATERCRESS
Refreshing, slightly peppery, dark green leaf vegetable commercially cultivated and also found wild in freshwater streams. Used primarily in salads and as a popular garnish.

Index

ACKNOWLEDGMENTS

The publishers would like to thank the following people and organizations for their generous assistance and support in producing this book:
Sharon C. Lott, Stephen W. Griswold, Tara Brown, Ken DellaPenta, the buyers for Gardener's Eden, and the buyers and
store managers for Pottery Barn and Williams-Sonoma stores.

The following kindly lent props for the photography:
Biordi Art Imports, J. Goldsmith Antiques, Fillamento, Fredericksen Hardware, Forrest Jones, Stephanie Greenleigh, Sue Fisher King,
Lorraine & Judson Puckett, Waterford/Wedgwood, Sue White and Chuck Williams.

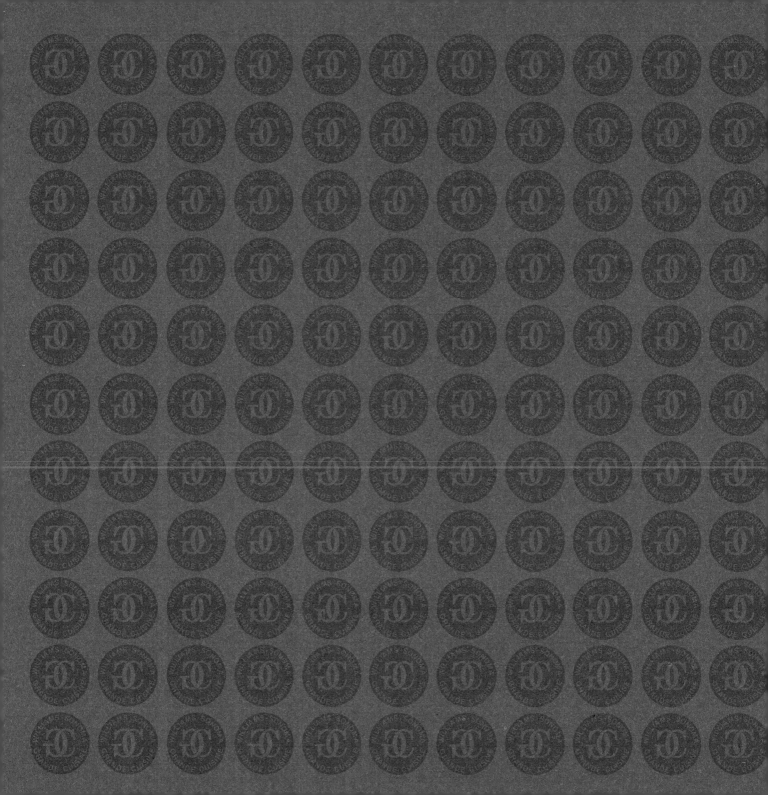